# Handstand Drills and Conditioning

## Karen M. Goeller

www.GymnasticsDrills.com

Gymnastics Drills and Conditioning
For the Handstand



Copyright © Goeller 2007


No part of this book may be reproduced in whole or in part in any form or by any means, electronic or mechanical including photocopying, recording, or by any information storage and retrieval system now known or hereafter invented without written permission from the author and publisher.
The Gymnastics Stuff and Strength Teacher Logos are the property of Gymnastics Stuff and may not be used or reproduced without the express written permission of Gymnastics Stuff.
Most of our books are also available at quantity discounts. For information please write to the author and publisher. Contact information can be found through the website, GymnasticsBooks.com.

ISBN: 978-0-6151-7724-3




Copyright © Goeller 2005

# Gymnastics Drills and Conditioning
## For the Handstand

This book includes drills and conditioning exercises that were used with Karen's athletes for many years.

Although the drills, when done correctly have proven challenging to gymnasts of all levels, they are most useful to the developing gymnasts in levels one through eight.

As the owner of a gymnastics club for nearly ten years and gymnastics coach for 25, Karen has spent thousands of hours coaching, teaching skills through progressions, drills, strength, and flexibility.

She considers it a privilege to have worked at Karolyi's Gymnastics Camp in Texas for seven summers as well as at US Gymnastics Training Camp held in Massachusetts and International Gymnastics Camp in Pennsylvania for a decade of Holiday Clinics.

Working at these camps along with attending many USA Gymnastics events such as Regional Congress and the National TOPS Training Camp have all been contributing factors to her vast knowledge of the sport. Karen has great appreciation for all those who were so generous with their knowledge, especially Paul Spadaro, Bela Karolyi, and Martha Karolyi.

www.GymnasticsDrills.com

## The Handstand is the most important skill in the sport of gymnastics and remaining tight is essential!

Gymnasts of all levels perform the handstand very often during the course of their workout. While performing many skills in gymnastics, the gymnast must actually pass through the handstand or vertical phase safely and efficiently. With a good handstand a gymnast should be able to build skills and therefore progress through the gymnastics levels safely and efficiently.

The handstand involves so many muscle groups working simultaneously that it is often difficult for the new gymnast to fully master the handstand prior to being expected to perform even more difficult skills. Often times, the enthusiasm level in many gymnastics clubs drives the coaches and athletes to move to more difficult skills prior to the mastery of those already introduced, such as the handstand.

Many new gymnasts have trouble keeping their abdominal section tight or their lower back in the correct position. Several of the drills and conditioning exercises shown in this book should help the gymnast learn to pull their lower abdominal section in while elongating their lower back for a straight and tight position.

This straight and tight position should first be learned lying down or standing up prior to expecting the new gymnast to hold the position upside down and with an open shoulder position. And before the actual shape of the handstand is learned, it is often best to teach the gymnast how to squeeze individual muscle groups, one at a time. The gymnast must first learn how to get tight and remain tight while lying on the floor, standing, and in every position in between before we can expect them to do that safely upside down and while in motion.

Copyright © Goeller 2005

# Gymnastics Drills and Conditioning
## For the Handstand

It is for that reason and for safety that a handful of these drills take place on the floor or while standing up. Many of these drills require a coach to spot their gymnast while other drills can be performed more independently and with minimal equipment.

Take it slow and be sure to pay attention to detail; the handstand is the most important skill in the sport of gymnastics!

Gymnastics Drills and Conditioning Exercises for the Handstand should be extremely helpful for beginning gymnasts just learning the handstand as well as the more advanced gymnasts in need of a friendly reminder on how to remain tight while performing skills involving or passing through the handstand.

These exercises are a necessity for all gymnasts!

# Contents

**The Squeeze**
7   Buttocks Squeeze
8   Buttocks Squeeze Elevated
9   Buttocks Squeeze Elevated – One Leg
10  Buttocks Squeeze and Lift
12  Squeeze, Lift, and Release One Leg
14  Squeeze, Lift, Passé Position

**The Squeeze in Motion**
17  Guided Lift to Stand
19  Guided Lift to Stand in Passé Position
21  Guided Lift to Stand in Horizontal Position
23  Guided Set Down
25  Guided Set Down in Passé Position
27  Guided Lift to Stand in Horizontal Position
29  Advanced Lean Back

**Pelvic Tilt**
31  Belly Lift
32  Belly Lift and Squeeze
33  Forearm Belly Lift
35  Elevated Forearm Belly Lift
37  Second Elevated Forearm Belly Lift
39  Third Elevated Forearm Belly Lift
41  Belly Button Lift on Wall

**Abdominal Control**
43  Octagon Rock
45  Octagon Tuck

Copyright © Goeller 2005

# Gymnastics Drills and Conditioning
# For the Handstand

### Shape and Shoulder Work
- 47  Rounded Push Up Position
- 49  Rainbow Shrug
- 51  Elevated Rainbow Shrug
- 53  Second Elevated Rainbow Shrug
- 55  Third Elevated Rainbow Shrug

### Handstand Production
- 57  Wall Climb
- 61  Handstand Shrug
- 63  Handstand Shrug Feet Together
- 65  Handstand – Tight and Stable
- 67  Handstand Tuck Open
- 69  Wall Handstand Tuck Open

### Shape in Motion
- 71  Rainbow Handstand Rainbow
- 75  Planche – Forward and Back
- 79  Planche – Handstand - Planche
- 83  Planche - Virtual Handstand - Planche
- 89  Handstand Shoulder Control

- 95  **Quick Review**

- 97  **Other Books by Author**

# The Squeeze

First we will separate the front from the back while learning to contract certain muscles necessary for body tightness.

**Buttocks Squeeze**
Have your gymnast lie on their back, face up.
Use the floor exercise area or a firm mat.
Once they are comfortable, have them place their arms at their sides and their palms down.
Next, instruct your gymnast to keep everything on the floor, including their hands, head, shoulder blades, buttocks, legs, and feet.
Once your gymnast is completely flat, instruct them to lift their buttocks off the floor, leaving everything else on the floor.
Instruct your gymnast to keep their shoulder blades and legs on the floor while they attempt to lift (squeeze) their buttocks.
Once lifted, your gymnast will have a small arch in their lower back. This is not for the positioning of a handstand; it is just a place to start with teaching a new gymnast to squeeze their buttocks in order to prevent or correct an angle or pike at the hip.

# Gymnastics Drills and Conditioning For the Handstand

**Buttocks Squeeze Elevated**

Once your gymnast is able to perform the **Buttocks Squeeze**, lifting their buttocks slightly off the floor successfully by squeezing the muscles, ask them to perform the same drill with their feet elevated on a mat approximately 4 inches high.

Have your gymnast lie on their back with their feet elevated on a folded mat or other object that is approximately 4 inches high. Instruct them to place their arms at their sides with their palms down.

Be sure the mat is soft enough so their heels are comfortable. Once your gymnast is in the starting position, instruct them to keep everything on the floor, including their hands, head, and shoulder blades.

Next, instruct your gymnast to lift their buttocks off the floor by squeezing those muscles.

It is not necessary that your gymnast intentionally arch, but they must squeeze their buttocks enough to completely open their hips so there is no hip angle\pike.

The demand to be placed on that muscle group has increased with the elevation making this drill slightly more difficult.

# The Squeeze

**Buttocks Squeeze Elevated – One Leg**

Now, your gymnast is ready for more of a challenge with this muscle group and exercise.

Have your gymnast lie on their back with their feet elevated on a folded mat or other object that is approximately 4 inches high. Instruct them to place their arms at their sides with their palms down.

Be sure the mat is soft enough so their heels are comfortable. Once your gymnast is in the starting position, instruct them to keep their hands, head, and shoulder blades on the floor throughout the exercise.

Next, instruct your gymnast to lift one foot an inch or two higher than the mat. Inform them they must keep that foot off the mat throughout the exercise.

Instruct your gymnast to keep both legs straight during this exercise.

Once in position with one foot higher than the mat, instruct your gymnast to lift their buttocks off the floor while keeping the lifted leg from touching the mat.

Your gymnast can place their arms in any position on the floor for balance.

Once your gymnast has performed the buttocks lift with one leg up in the air, instruct them to perform the exercise with the other foot up in the air. This drill may be a challenge for many gymnasts, even the more experienced gymnasts!

# Gymnastics Drills and Conditioning
# For the Handstand

We will now perform a set of drills involving the same muscle groups, but we will ask your gymnast to remain tight while in motion.

It is only possible to perform this set of drills with a coach physically spotting your gymnast.

### Buttocks Squeeze and Lift

Instruct your gymnast to lie on their back, face up.
Use the floor exercise area or a firm mat.
Once they are comfortable, have them place their arms at their sides and their palms down.
Next, instruct your gymnast to keep everything on the floor, including their hands, head, shoulder blades, buttocks, legs, and feet.
Once your gymnast is completely flat, instruct them to squeeze their buttocks, as they did in the first few exercises in this book. Tell your gymnast they will be expected to keep the tight\squeezed position throughout the rest of the exercise.
Instruct your gymnast to keep their shoulder blades and hands on the floor while you lift their feet approximately 4-6 inches off the floor.
Many gymnasts will drop their buttocks as soon as you attempt to lift their feet. It often takes 2-3 attempts for the gymnast to have the ability to hold the squeezed position while in motion.
If your gymnast immediately drops their buttocks, just ask them to squeeze again and hold the squeeze while you lift their feet up again.
Once lifted, your gymnast may have a small arch in their lower back. This is not for the positioning of a handstand; it is again just a place to start with while teaching a new gymnast to squeeze their buttocks in order to prevent or correct an angle at the hip\a pike.

Once your gymnast has mastered the **Squeeze in Motion**, they are ready for the next exercise. Be sure your gymnast can remain straight, keeping their buttocks off the floor, for at least 10

## The Squeeze

seconds prior to moving to the next step in the Squeeze Group of exercises.

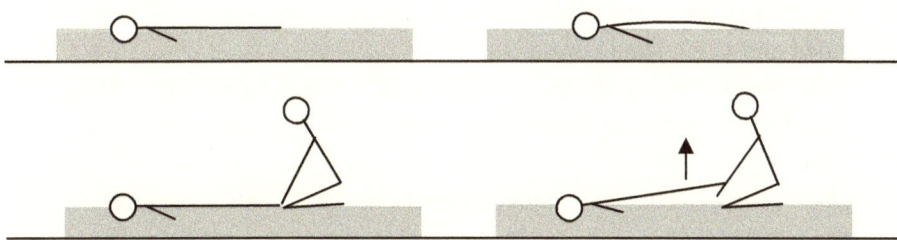

**Squeeze and Lower**
If the **Squeeze and Lift** is too difficult for the new gymnast to comprehend, perform it in the **reverse**.
Lift your gymnast's feet approximately 4-6 inches off the floor.
Next, instruct them to lift their buttocks off the floor.
Inform your gymnast they will be expected to remain straight until their heels touch the floor.
Next, slowly lower your gymnast's feet toward the floor, constantly reminding them to keep their buttocks off the floor.
Once your gymnast can perform the exercise in reverse, as just described, have them try the **Squeeze and Lift** again starting with everything flat on the floor, squeezing their buttocks, and then having their heels lifted by the coach.
Remember, your gymnast's body must move as one unit, remaining tight, and preventing their buttocks from collapsing.

See how many times your gymnast can be lifted and lowered without allowing their buttocks to collapse. Connecting 6-10 without their buttocks collapsing is a reasonable goal.

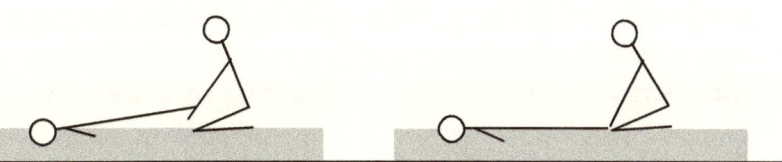

# Gymnastics Drills and Conditioning
## For the Handstand

**Squeeze, Lift, and Release One Leg**

Instruct your gymnast to lie on their back, face up.
Use the floor exercise area or a firm mat.
Once they are comfortable, have them place their arms at their sides and their palms down.
Next, instruct your gymnast to be sure everything is on the floor, including their hands, head, shoulder blades, buttocks, legs, and feet.
Once your gymnast is completely flat, instruct them to squeeze their buttocks.
Inform them that they will be expected to keep the tight position throughout the rest of the exercise as they did in the previous exercise.
Tell your gymnast you will release one foot and they must keep their feet and legs together even after one of their feet is no longer being supported.
You are now only holding one of your gymnast's feet while they squeeze their legs together enough to prevent the unsupported foot from falling to the floor.
Remind your gymnast to focus on keeping their legs together and buttocks off the floor throughout this exercise.
Now your gymnast is performing two tasks simultaneously, squeezing their buttocks and keeping their legs together!
If your gymnast is able to remain in the squeezed position for a few seconds return the support to both feet and then release the support from the other foot while they are still 4-6 inches off the floor.
It often takes 2-3 attempts for the gymnast to have the ability to hold the squeezed position while in motion and then keep their legs together while only one leg is supported.
Once lifted, your gymnast may still have a small arch in their lower back. This is not for the positioning of a handstand; it is again a place to start with teaching a new gymnast to squeeze their buttocks and keep their legs together simultaneously.

## The Squeeze

Remember, your gymnast's body must move as one unit, remaining tight, and preventing their buttocks from collapsing and their legs from separating.
See how many times your gymnast can be lifted and lowered without allowing their buttocks to collapse.

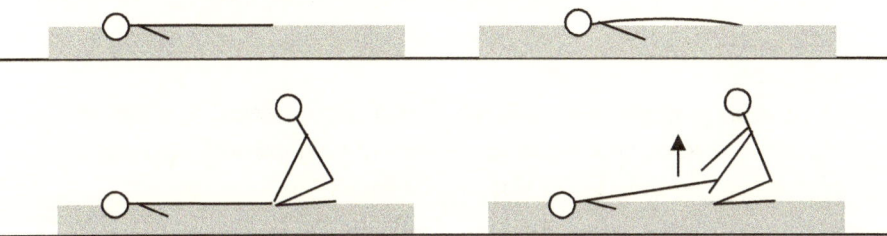

**Squeeze, Lift, One Leg**
You can **increase the difficulty** of the previous exercise by having your gymnast lie flat on their back again and inform them that they must squeeze their legs together from the start in addition to squeezing their buttocks.
Rather than lifting both feet from the start, lift only one foot and remind your gymnast the other foot and leg must rise with the supported foot.
Remember, your gymnast's body must move as one unit. They must remain tight and prevent their buttocks from collapsing and their legs from separating.
See how many times your gymnast can be lifted and lowered without allowing their buttocks to collapse.

# Gymnastics Drills and Conditioning
## For the Handstand

**Squeeze, Lift, Passé Position**

Instruct your gymnast to lie on their back, face up.
Use the floor exercise area or a firm mat.
Once they are comfortable, have them place their arms at their sides and their palms down.
Next, instruct your gymnast to start with everything on the floor, including their hands, head, shoulder blades, buttocks, legs, and feet.
Once your gymnast is completely flat, instruct them to bend one leg so their knee is pointed up toward the ceiling and the bottom of the foot on that leg is flat on the floor.
Once your gymnast has one knee bent, instruct them to lift that heel off the floor and point their toe, placing their big toe next to their knee. This position is commonly called the passé position in dance.
Once your gymnast's leg is in the passé position, ask them to squeeze their buttocks and squeeze their legs in that position.
If you instruct your gymnast to think of squeezing their thighs together even though their legs are positioned this way and to press their toe against the side of their knee, they should be able to hold the passé position throughout the exercise.
Remind your gymnast again that they will be expected to keep the tight passé position throughout the rest of the exercise.
Instruct your gymnast to keep their shoulder blades and hands on the floor while you lift the heel\foot of the straight leg approximately 4-6 inches off the floor.
Remind your gymnast to continue to squeeze their buttocks while holding the passé position until you lower their leg back down to the floor.
Your gymnast is performing two tasks simultaneously, squeezing their buttocks and holding that passé position!
Once lifted, your gymnast may still have a small arch in their lower back. This is not for the positioning of a handstand or full turn; it is just a place to start with teaching a new gymnast to squeeze their buttocks and keep their legs in an assigned position.

## The Squeeze

Remember, your gymnast's body must move as one unit. They must remain tight and prevent their buttocks from collapsing and their legs from separating.

See how many times your gymnast can be lifted and lowered without allowing their buttocks to collapse or releasing the passé position.

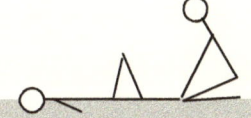 

This drill can be performed with the free leg straight and at hip height for the most advanced gymnasts.

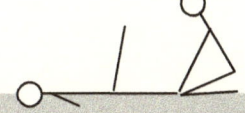 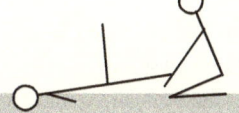

# The Squeeze in Motion

The previous drills allowed the gymnast to keep their upper body on the floor while performing each exercise. The next few drills will require the gymnast to keep their feet on the floor while their upper body is in motion, going to and from the standing and lying down positions.

Again, your gymnast will be required to squeeze their buttocks area and keep their legs in assigned positions

**Guided Lift to Stand**
Instruct your gymnast to lie on their back, face up.
For this and many drills to follow we strongly recommend you use a "**Marshmallow Mat**" or other Pit type mat.
(Marshmallow Mat information is on page 97)
Once your gymnast is comfortable, have them place their arms at their sides with their palms on their thighs.
Next, instruct your gymnast to start with everything on the floor, including their head, shoulder blades, buttocks, legs, and feet.
Once your gymnast is completely flat, instruct them to squeeze their buttocks.
Remind your gymnast that they will be expected to keep the tight position throughout the rest of the exercise.
Once your gymnast is tight and ready, you will place your hands under their shoulder blades or armpits.
Be sure to place your hands far down enough that it will be safe enough to lift your gymnast up to their feet.
It is recommended to use an assistant to help spot the larger gymnasts with this drill.
Once ready, carefully lift your gymnast to their feet.
In order to prevent incorrect technique and injury, do not continue to lift your gymnast if they are not tight when they reach 4-6 inches from the floor.

Copyright © Goeller 2005

# Gymnastics Drills and Conditioning
## For the Handstand

Many gymnasts need 2-3 attempts before they can perform this drill successfully. If a gymnast appears to begin sitting up rather than having their body move as one unit, slowly lower them back down to the mat to start the drill over again.

Be very careful with the smaller gymnasts. If you lift them too quickly they can fall forward and to their face. You should use a second coach to supervise the top portion of the drill in order to prevent your gymnast from passing through the standing position and falling forward.

It may appear that your gymnast will have a small arch in their lower back until they reach the standing position. This is not for the positioning of a handstand. This drill is for the purpose of teaching a new gymnast to squeeze their buttocks while in motion.

Remember, your gymnast's body must move as one unit. They must remain tight and prevent their buttocks from collapsing toward the floor.

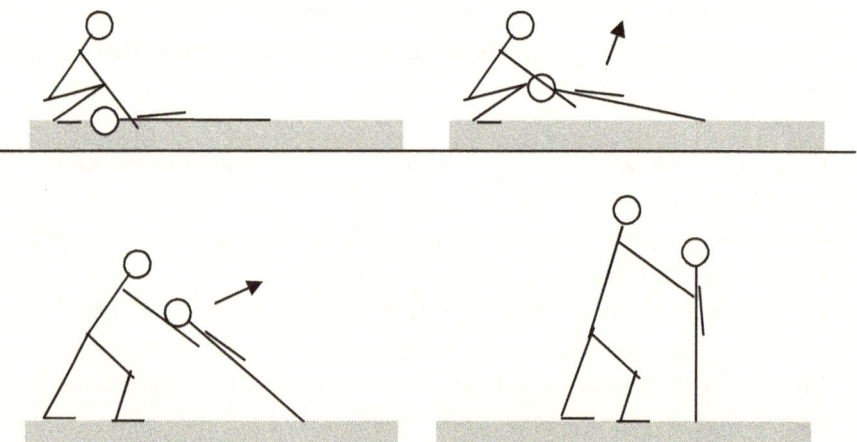

www.GymnasticsDrills.com

# The Squeeze in Motion

**Guided Lift to Stand – Passé Position**
Instruct your gymnast to lie on their back, face up.
For this drill we strongly recommend you use a "Marshmallow Mat" or other Pit type mat.
Once your gymnast is comfortable, have them place their arms at their sides with their palms on their thighs.
Next, instruct your gymnast to start with everything on the floor, including their head, shoulder blades, buttocks, legs, and feet.
Once your gymnast is completely flat, instruct them to bend one leg so their knee is pointed up toward the ceiling and the bottom of their foot is flat on the floor.
Once your gymnast has one knee bent, instruct them to lift that heel off the floor and point their toe, placing their big toe next to their knee. This position is commonly called the passé position in dance.
Once your gymnast's leg is in the passé position, ask them to squeeze their buttocks and squeeze their legs in that position.
If you instruct your gymnast to think of squeezing their thighs together even though their legs are positioned this way and to press their toe against the side of their knee, they should be able to hold the passé position throughout the exercise.
Remind your gymnast again that they will be expected to keep the tight passé position throughout the rest of the exercise.
Once your gymnast has been instructed, you must then place your hands on your gymnast's shoulder blades or just under their armpits in order to be able to securely lift them to the standing position.
Once ready, you must carefully lift your gymnast to their feet. In order to prevent incorrect technique and injury, do not continue to lift your gymnast if they are not tight when they reach 3-4 inches from the floor.
Many gymnasts need 2-3 attempts before they can perform this drill successfully. If a gymnast appears to begin sitting up rather than having their body move as one unit, slowly lower them back down to the mat to start the drill over again.

# Gymnastics Drills and Conditioning
## For the Handstand

Be very careful with the smaller gymnasts. If you lift them too quickly they can fall forward and to their face. You should use a second coach to supervise the top portion of the drill in order to prevent your gymnast from passing through the standing position and falling forward.

Remind your gymnast to continue to squeeze their buttocks while holding the passé position until they are completely standing for at least 5 seconds.

Your gymnast is performing two tasks simultaneously, squeezing their buttocks and holding that passé position!

Once lifted, your gymnast may still have a small arch in their lower back at first. This is not as much for the positioning of a handstand or full turn as it is a place to start with teaching a new gymnast to squeeze their buttocks and keep their legs in an assigned position.

Remember, your gymnast's body must move as one unit. They must remain tight and prevent their buttocks from collapsing toward the floor.

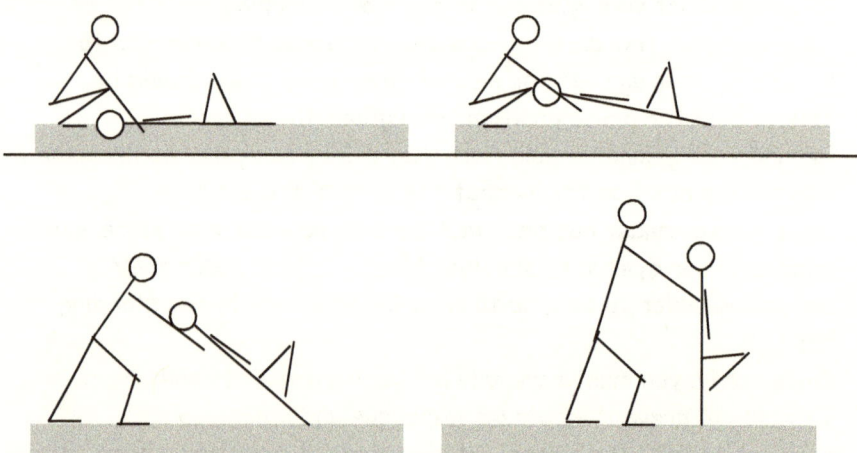

## The Squeeze in Motion

**Guided Lift to Stand – Leg at Horizontal**
This drill can be performed with the free leg straight and at hip height for the more advanced gymnasts.
Instruct your gymnast to lie on their back, face up.
For this drill we strongly recommend you use a "Marshmallow Mat" or other Pit type mat.
Once your gymnast is comfortable, have them place their arms to a side middle position with their palms on the floor.
Next, instruct your gymnast to start with everything on the floor, including their hands, head, shoulder blades, buttocks, legs, and feet.
Once your gymnast is completely flat, instruct them to lift one leg so their toe is pointed up toward the ceiling.
Once your gymnast's leg is in the correct position, ask them to squeeze their buttocks and squeeze their legs in that position.
If you instruct your gymnast to think of squeezing their thighs together even though their legs are positioned this way, they should be able to hold the leg position throughout the exercise.
Remind your gymnast again that they will be expected to keep the tight position throughout the rest of the exercise.
Once your gymnast has been instructed, you must then place your hands on your gymnast's shoulder blades or just under their armpits in order to be able to securely lift your gymnast to the standing position.
Once ready, you must carefully lift your gymnast to their feet. In order to prevent incorrect technique and injury, do not continue to lift your gymnast if they are not tight when they reach 3-4 inches from the floor.
Many gymnasts need 2-3 attempts before they can perform this drill successfully. If a gymnast appears to begin sitting up rather than having their body move as one unit, slowly lower them back down to the mat to start the drill over again.
Be very careful with the smaller gymnasts. If you lift them too quickly they can fall forward and to their face. You should use a second coach to supervise the top portion of the drill in order to prevent your gymnast from passing through the standing position and falling forward.

# Gymnastics Drills and Conditioning
## For the Handstand

Remind your gymnast to continue to squeeze their buttocks while holding the correct position until they are completely standing for at least 5 seconds. Their leg must still be up, at hip height. Your gymnast is performing two tasks simultaneously, squeezing their buttocks and holding their leg in an assigned position!
Once lifted, your gymnast may still have a small arch in their lower back at first. This is not as much for the positioning of a handstand or full turn as it is a place to start with teaching a new gymnast to squeeze their buttocks and keep their legs in an assigned position.
Remember, your gymnast's body must move as one unit. They must remain tight and prevent their buttocks from collapsing toward the floor.

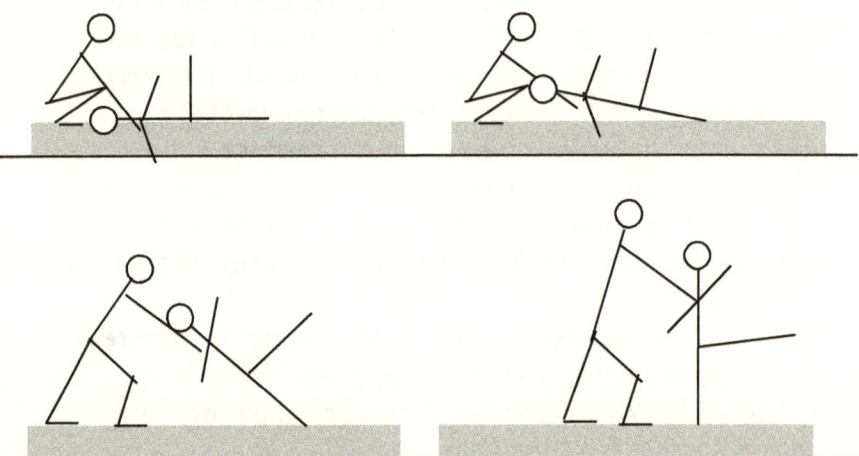

## The Squeeze in Motion

**Guided Set Down**

Have your gymnast stand in front of a "Marshmallow Mat" or other Pit type mat. It must be a very soft mat that will not bottom out.

Once your gymnast is standing in front of the mat instruct them to turn so that their back is facing the mat.

You must then stand behind your gymnast and be ready to completely spot your gymnast.

Once you and your gymnast are in position, instruct your gymnast to place their arms at their sides and squeeze their buttocks. Inform your gymnast that they will be expected to keep the tight position, remaining straight, throughout the rest of the exercise. Many gymnasts will respond to cues such as remain as stiff as a board or stay straight and tall like a soldier.

Once your gymnast has been instructed, you must then place your hands on your gymnast's shoulder blades or just under their armpits in order to be able to securely and slowly lower your gymnast down to the pit type mat.

Once you have a firm grip and are completely ready, instruct your gymnast to lean back into your hands and remain very tight as you lower them to the mat.

In order to prevent incorrect technique and injury, do not continue to lower your gymnast if they are not tight when they begin this exercise.

Many gymnasts will need 2-3 attempts before they can remain totally straight from the standing position all the way down to the lying position. You must be ready at all times in the event your gymnast falls or collapses. Many gymnasts will drop their buttocks to the mat in their first attempt to be lowered completely.

Remember, your gymnast's body must move as one unit. They must remain tight and prevent their buttocks from collapsing toward the floor.

# Gymnastics Drills and Conditioning
## For the Handstand

# The Squeeze in Motion

**Guided Set Down - Passé Position**
Have your gymnast stand in front of a "Marshmallow Mat" or other Pit type mat. It must be a very soft mat that will not bottom out.
Once your gymnast is standing in front of the mat instruct them to turn so that their back is facing the mat.
You must stand behind your gymnast and be ready to completely spot them.
Once you and your gymnast are in position, instruct your gymnast to place their arms at their sides and squeeze their buttocks.
Next, instruct them to bend one leg so their knee is lifted to hip height and their big toe is next to their knee.
This position is commonly called the passé position in dance.
Once your gymnast's leg is in the passé position, ask them to squeeze their buttocks and squeeze their legs in that position.
If you instruct them to think of squeezing their thighs together even though their legs are positioned this way and to press their toe against the side of their knee, they should be able to hold the passé position throughout the exercise.
Remind your gymnast again that they will be expected to keep the tight position throughout the rest of the exercise.
Many gymnasts will respond to cues such as remain as stiff as a board or stay straight and tall like a soldier, even though one knee is up.
Once your gymnast has been instructed, you must then place your hands on your gymnast's shoulder blades or just under your gymnast's armpits in order to be able to securely and slowly lower them down to the pit type mat.
Once you have a firm grip and are completely ready, instruct your gymnast to lean back into your hands and remain very tight as you lower them to the mat.
Be sure to remind your gymnast to hold the passé position throughout this exercise.
Many gymnasts will need 2-3 attempts before they can remain totally straight from the standing position all the way down to the lying position. You must be ready at all times in the event your gymnast falls or collapses. Many gymnasts will drop their

# Gymnastics Drills and Conditioning
## For the Handstand

buttocks to the mat in their first attempt to be lowered completely.

Remember, your gymnast's body must move as one unit. They must remain tight and prevent their buttocks from collapsing toward the floor.

# The Squeeze in Motion

**Guided Set Down – Leg at Horizontal**
This drill can be performed with the free leg straight and at hip height for the more advanced gymnasts.
Have your gymnast stand in front of a "Marshmallow Mat" or other Pit type mat. It must be a very soft mat that will not bottom out.
Once your gymnast is standing in front of the mat instruct them to turn so that their back is facing the mat.
You must stand behind your gymnast and be ready to completely spot them.
Once you and your gymnast are in position, instruct your gymnast to hold their arms at a side middle position and squeeze their buttocks.
Next, instruct them to lift one leg so their knee and toe are lifted to hip height.
Once your gymnast's leg is hip height, ask them to squeeze their buttocks and squeeze their legs in that position.
If you instruct your gymnast to think of squeezing their thighs together even though their legs are positioned this way, they should be able to hold the leg position throughout the exercise.
Remind your gymnast again that they will be expected to keep the tight position throughout the rest of the exercise.
Many gymnasts will respond to cues such as remain as stiff as a board or stay straight and tall like a soldier, even though one leg is up.
Once your gymnast has been instructed, you must then place your hands on your gymnast's shoulder blades or just under their armpits in order to be able to securely and slowly lower them down to the pit type mat.
Once you have a firm grip and are completely ready, instruct your gymnast to lean back into your hands and remain very tight as you lower them to the mat.
Be sure to remind your gymnast to hold the leg position throughout this exercise.
Many gymnasts will need 2-3 attempts before they can remain totally straight from the standing position all the way down to the lying position. You must be ready at all times in the event

## Gymnastics Drills and Conditioning
## For the Handstand

your gymnast falls or collapses. Many gymnasts will drop their buttocks to the mat in their first attempt to be lowered completely.

Remember, your gymnast's body must move as one unit. They must remain tight and prevent their buttocks from collapsing toward the floor.

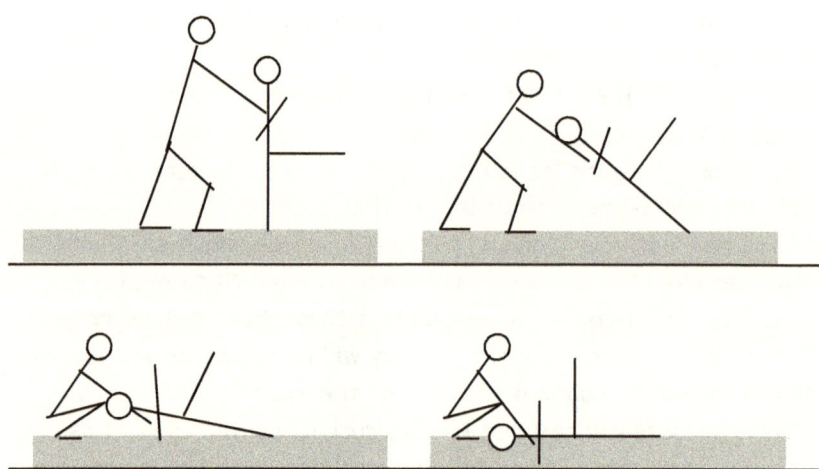

The Squeeze in Motion

**Advanced Lean Back**
**This is a very advanced drill used in dance as well as gymnastics for body tightness.**

The coach\spotter, must be very experienced and extremely strong in order to spot this drill safely. It is impossible for a gymnast to perform this drill successfully without an extremely good spotter.
Place a "Marshmallow" or Pit type mat behind your gymnast in case they become loose and fall.
Have your gymnast's back facing the mat
Instruct your gymnast to lift their leg so that you can securely wrap both of your hands around your gymnast's ankle.
You must then step (w\o shoes on) on or in front of your gymnast's foot (on the supporting leg) in order to prevent them from slipping or falling during this exercise.
Instruct your gymnast to squeeze their buttocks, stand very tall, lift their arms to a side middle position, and then lean back holding the straight\tight body. While your gymnast is leaning back, you are holding your gymnast's leg in order to slowly guide them to the mat and then return them to the upright\standing position.
While your gymnast remains extremely tight hold their ankle and lower them towards the mat.
Once your gymnast comes close to the mat, you then raise\pull them back up to the starting position, standing with one leg at hip height with their arms at a side middle position.
You must continually remind your gymnast to stay tight and tall even though they are only being supported by one leg.
Your gymnast must keep a straight line from their head to the supporting foot, and their arms side/middle. Their body must lower and rise as a unit.
This is the **very advanced** method of performing the **Guided Set Down** because your gymnast is not only expected to keep their buttocks squeezed, they are expected to remain tight in their legs, keep the position, and balance.

# Gymnastics Drills and Conditioning
## For the Handstand

*In fond and loving memory of Renville Duncan. Our Choreographer and so much more...*

# Pelvic Tilt

Now we will work on squeezing the muscles in front of the body such as the abdominal muscles as well as begin to teach the correct shape for the handstand position. Once the correct shape is established, you will teach your gymnast to hold the correct shape while in motion.

**Belly Button Lift**
Have your gymnast lie on their stomach, face down.
Use the floor exercise area or a firm mat.
Once they are comfortable, have them place their arms up by their ears, keeping their arms straight.
Ask your gymnast to rest their wrists and hands on the floor.
Next, instruct your gymnast to keep everything on the floor, including their wrists, chin, armpits, chest, hips, thighs, and feet.
Once your gymnast is completely flat, instruct them to lift their belly button off the floor, leaving everything else on the floor.
Remind your gymnast again to keep their armpits, chest, hips, and feet down while they lift their belly button.
Once your gymnast lifts their belly button you will see their lower back elongate into the correct position for a handstand.
Their buttocks should be under once their belly button is lifted off the floor.
Your gymnast has just begun to learn the "**pelvic tilt!**"
Have your gymnast relax and then repeat this drill several times.
Make sure they keep everything on the floor with the exception of their belly button once lifted.

Once your gymnast has learned how to lift their belly button without lifting anything else, ask them to stretch as long as they can before they lift their belly button so they can better understand the shape of the proper handstand.

The illustration for this drill is very general.

Gymnastics Drills and Conditioning
For the Handstand

**Belly Button Lift and Squeeze the Buttocks**
Once the idea of lifting their belly button is introduced to your gymnast, they are ready to more closely simulate the shape for a handstand.
Have your gymnast lie on their stomach, face down.
Use the floor exercise area or a firm mat. Once they are comfortable, have them place their arms up by their ears, keeping their arms straight.
Ask your gymnast to rest their wrists and hands on the floor. Next, instruct your gymnast to keep everything on the floor, including their wrists, chin, armpits, chest, hips, thighs, and feet.
Once your gymnast is completely flat, instruct them to squeeze their buttocks as they did in the **Buttocks Squeeze** (P. 7) and then to lift their belly button off the floor as they did in the **Belly Button Lift**. (P. 31)
Everything else must still remain on the floor once their belly button is lifted along with their buttocks being squeezed.
Remind your gymnast again to keep their armpits, chest, hips, and feet down while they squeeze their buttocks and lift their belly button.
Once your gymnast lifts their belly button and squeezes their buttocks you will see their lower back elongate into the correct position for a handstand.
Your gymnast should begin to feel and perform the correct shape in their lower body for a handstand.
Your gymnast's buttocks should be tucked under once their belly button is lifted off the floor.
Your gymnast has learned the "**pelvic tilt**" with the **Buttocks Squeeze**.

## Pelvic Tilt

Have your gymnast relax and then repeat the drill several times. Make sure they keep everything on the floor with the exception of their belly button once lifted.

Once your gymnast has learned how to squeeze their buttocks and then lift their belly button without lifting anything else, ask them to stretch as long as they can before they lift their belly button so they can better understand the shape of the proper handstand.

The illustration for this drill is very general.

**Forearm Support and Belly Button Lift**
Have your gymnast lie on their stomach, face down.
Use the floor exercise area or a firm mat.
Once your gymnast is on the floor, have them place their elbows underneath their armpits, so they can perform a forearm support.
A forearm support is a push up position, but resting on the forearms.
Your gymnast's legs, hips, and chest all come up off the floor once they are in the forearm support.
Instruct your gymnast to point their feet rather than keeping them flexed with the ball of their feet on the floor. Keeping their feet pointed puts more of a demand on your gymnast's abdominal muscles.
Ask your gymnast to keep their wrists, elbows, and palms on the floor for this exercise.
Next, instruct your gymnast to start with their body straight. Once your gymnast is completely straight, instruct them to squeeze their buttocks as they did in the **Buttocks Squeeze.** (P. 7) Once in the forearm support with their buttocks squeezed, instruct your gymnast to pull their belly button in just as if they

# Gymnastics Drills and Conditioning
## For the Handstand

were lifting their belly button off the floor in the **Belly Button Lift**. (P. 31)

You should see the lower portion of your gymnast's back elongate into the correct position for a handstand.

Once your gymnast squeezes their buttocks and pulls their belly button in they should begin to feel and perform the correct shape in their lower body for a handstand.

Your gymnast's buttocks should be tucked under once their belly button is pulled in.

Your gymnast has just performed the "pelvic tilt" and **Buttocks Squeeze** on their forearms.

Be sure your gymnast's head remains neutral throughout the exercise.

Be sure your gymnast's legs remain straight throughout the exercise.

Have your gymnast relax and then repeat the drill several times. Make sure they start straight and then form the correct shape with their lower body.

Once your gymnast has learned how to squeeze their buttocks and then pull their belly button in without changing anything else, you can ask them to push down on the floor (shrug) and pull in their chest so the portion of their back between their shoulder blades becomes rounded and more closely forms the shape necessary for a good handstand. (P. 47)

Your gymnast will first squeeze their buttocks, pull in their belly button, then push down on the floor with their forearms and pull in their chest so they can better understand the shape of the proper handstand.

The illustration for this drill is very general.

## Pelvic Tilt

**Elevated Belly Button Lift on Forearms**
Have your gymnast lie on their stomach, face down.
Use the floor exercise area or a firm mat.
Place a folded panel mat near their feet so that your gymnast can place their feet on the mat which is 8-12 inches high.
Instruct your gymnast to place the top portion of their feet and ankles on the mat. They can place part of their shin on the mat as well if it is more comfortable.
Once your gymnast is on the floor with their feet on a mat, have them place their elbows underneath their armpits, so they can perform a forearm support\push up type position.
A forearm support is a push up position, but resting on the forearms.
Your gymnast's legs, hips, and chest all come up off the floor once they are in the forearm support.
Ask your gymnast to keep their wrists, elbows, and palms on the floor.
Next, instruct your gymnast to start with their body and legs straight.
Once your gymnast is completely straight with their feet on the mat, instruct them to squeeze their buttocks.
Once in the forearm support with their buttocks squeezed, instruct your gymnast to pull their belly button in just as if they were lifting their belly button off the floor in the **Belly Button Lift.** (P. 31)
You should see the lower portion of your gymnast's back elongate into the correct position for a handstand.
Once your gymnast squeezes their buttocks and pulls in their belly button they should begin to feel and perform the correct shape in their lower body for a handstand.
Your gymnast's buttocks should be tucked under once their belly button is pulled in.
Your gymnast has just performed the "pelvic tilt" on their forearms and elevated.
Be sure your gymnast's head remains neutral throughout the exercise.

# Gymnastics Drills and Conditioning
## For the Handstand

Be sure your gymnast's legs remain straight throughout the exercise.

Have your gymnast relax and then repeat the drill several times. Make sure they start straight and then form the correct shape with their lower body.

Once your gymnast has learned how to squeeze their buttocks and then pull their belly button in without changing anything else, ask them to push down on the floor (shrug) and pull in their chest so the portion of their back between their shoulder blades becomes rounded and more closely forms the shape necessary for a good handstand. (P. 47)

Your gymnast will first squeeze their buttocks, pull in their belly button, then push down on the floor with their forearms and pull in their chest so they can better understand the shape of the proper handstand. Of course, make sure they keep their knees straight the entire time.

The elevation increases and changes the demand on your gymnast's abdominal and upper body muscles.

The illustration for this drill is very general.

# Pelvic Tilt

**Second Elevated Belly Button Lift on Forearms**
Place a spotting block which is 24 to 32 inches high (or two – three panel mats) on the floor so that your gymnast can place their feet on the block for this exercise.
Instruct your gymnast to stand with their back to the block. Next, have them place their hands on the floor and then one foot on the block. Once they have one foot on the block, your gymnast can go down to their forearms and then place their other foot on the block.
They can also place part of their shin on the block as well if it is more comfortable for them.
Your gymnast should now be in a forearm support with their feet on the block.
Your gymnast's legs, hips, and chest should be off the floor at this time.
Ask your gymnast to keep their elbows, and palms on the floor.
Next, instruct your gymnast to start with their body and legs straight.
Once your gymnast is completely straight with their feet on the block, instruct them to squeeze their buttocks.
Once in the forearm support with their buttocks squeezed, instruct your gymnast to pull their belly button in just as if they were lifting their belly button off the floor in the **Belly Button Lift.** (P. 31)
You should see the lower portion of your gymnast's back elongate into the correct position for a handstand.
Once your gymnast squeezes their buttocks and pulls their belly button in they should begin to feel and perform the correct shape in their lower body for a handstand.
Your gymnast's buttocks should be tucked under once their belly button is pulled in.
Your gymnast has just performed the "pelvic tilt" on their forearms and elevated.
Be sure your gymnast's head remains neutral throughout the exercise.
Be sure your gymnast's legs remain straight throughout the exercise.

# Gymnastics Drills and Conditioning
# For the Handstand

Have your gymnast relax and then repeat this drill several times. Make sure they start straight and then form the correct shape with their lower body.

Once your gymnast has learned how to squeeze their buttocks and then pull their belly button in without changing anything else, ask them to push down on the floor (shrug) and pull in their chest so the portion of their back between their shoulder blades becomes rounded and more closely forms the shape necessary for a good handstand. (P. 47)

Your gymnast will first squeeze their buttocks, then pull in their belly button, push down on the floor with their forearms (shrug) and pull in their chest so they can better understand the shape of the proper handstand. Of course, make sure they keep their knees straight the entire time.

The elevation increases and changes the demand again on your gymnast's abdominal and upper body muscles. With each increase in elevation there is an increase in demand on upper body muscles because more weight is being supported by the upper body rather than it being more evenly distributed as in a very low or no elevation.

The illustration for this drill is very general.

# Pelvic Tilt

**Third Elevated Belly Button Lift on Forearms**
Place a spotting block which is 36-48 inches high (or three - four panel mats) on the floor so that your gymnast can place their feet on the block for this exercise. If you are using a spotting block then just flip it up to the upright position.
A balance beam can also be used, but it will not feel as comfortable on your gymnast's feet.
Instruct your gymnast to stand with their back to the block.
Next, have them place their hands on the floor and then one foot on the block. Once they have one foot on the block, your gymnast can go down to their forearms and then place their other foot on the block.
Your gymnast can also place part of their shin on the block if it is more comfortable for them.
Your gymnast should now be in a forearm support with their feet on the block.
Your gymnast's legs, hips, and chest should be off the floor at this time.
Ask your gymnast to keep their elbows, and palms on the floor.
Next, instruct your gymnast to start with their body and legs straight.
Once your gymnast is completely straight with their feet on the block, instruct them to squeeze their buttocks.
Once in the forearm support with their buttocks squeezed, instruct your gymnast to pull their belly button in just as if they were lifting their belly button off the floor in the **Belly Button Lift.** (P. 31)
You should see the lower portion of your gymnast's back elongate into the correct position for a handstand.
Once your gymnast squeezes their buttocks and pulls their belly button in they should begin to feel and perform the correct shape in their lower body for a handstand.
Your gymnast's buttocks should be tucked under once their belly button is pulled in.
Your gymnast has just performed the "pelvic tilt" on their forearms and elevated.

# Gymnastics Drills and Conditioning
## For the Handstand

Be sure your gymnast's head remains neutral throughout the exercise.

Be sure your gymnast's legs remain straight throughout the exercise.

Have your gymnast relax and then repeat the drill several times. Make sure they start straight and then form the correct shape with their lower body.

Once your gymnast has learned how to squeeze their buttocks and then pull their belly button in without changing anything else, ask them to push down on the floor (shrug) and pull in their chest so the portion of their back between their shoulder blades becomes rounded and more closely forms the shape necessary for a good handstand. (P. 47)

Your gymnast will first squeeze their buttocks, pull in their belly button, then push down on the floor with their forearms (shrug) and pull in their chest so they can better understand the shape of the proper handstand. Of course, make sure they keep their knees straight the entire time.

The elevation increases and changes the demand on your gymnast's abdominal and upper body muscles. At this point, much of the demand will be on your gymnast's upper body because more weight is being supported by the upper body rather than it being more evenly distributed as in a very low or no elevation.

The illustration for this drill is very general.

# Pelvic Tilt

**Belly Button Lift with Feet on Wall**
Have your gymnast stand in front of a padded wall.
Make sure the padding or mat will not fall over onto your gymnast.
Instruct your gymnast to stand with their back to the wall and approximately 1-2 feet from the wall, depending on their height. Next, have them place their hands on the floor and then one foot on the wall. Once they have one (pointed) foot on the wall, your gymnast can go down to their forearms and then place their other foot on the wall. You can choose to have your gymnast remain on their hands for this exercise.
Your gymnast should now be in a forearm support or semi handstand with their feet on the wall.
Your gymnast's legs, hips, and chest should be off the floor and away from the wall at this time.
Ask your gymnast to keep their elbows and palms on the floor if they are using the forearm support.
Next, instruct your gymnast to start with their body and legs straight.
Once your gymnast is completely straight with their feet on the wall, instruct them to squeeze their buttocks.
Once in the forearm or hand support with their buttocks squeezed, instruct your gymnast to pull their belly button in just as if they were lifting their belly button off the floor in the **Belly Button Lift**. (P. 31)
You should see the lower portion of your gymnast's back elongate into the correct position for a handstand.
Once your gymnast squeezes their buttocks and pulls their belly button in they should begin to feel and perform the correct shape in their lower body for a handstand.
Your gymnast's buttocks should be tucked under once their belly button is pulled in.
Your gymnast has just performed the "pelvic tilt" on their forearms or elevated to nearly a handstand.
Have your gymnast relax and then repeat the drill a few times. Make sure they start straight and then form the correct shape with their lower body.

# Gymnastics Drills and Conditioning
# For the Handstand

Once your gymnast has learned how to squeeze their buttocks and then pull their belly button in without changing anything else, ask them to push down on the floor (shrug) and pull in their chest so the portion of their back between their shoulder blades becomes rounded and more closely forms the shape necessary for a good handstand. (P. 47)

Your gymnast will first squeeze their buttocks, pull in their belly button, then push down on the floor with their forearms or hands (shrug) and pull in their chest so they can better understand the shape of the proper handstand. Of course, make sure they keep their knees straight and head neutral the entire time.

The elevation increases and changes the demand on your gymnast's abdominal and upper body muscles. At this point, nearly all of the demand will be on your gymnast's upper body because much of their weight is being supported by the upper body rather than it being more evenly distributed as in a very low or no elevation.

The illustration for this drill is very general.

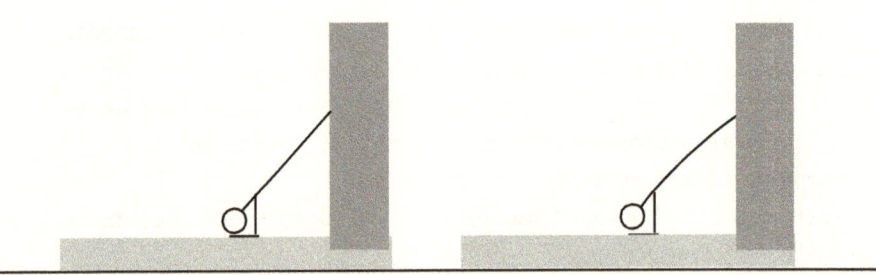

# Abdominal Control

**Octagon Rocks**
This is an abdominal conditioning and body tightness drill.
Have your gymnast stand in front of an octagon or barrel type mat.
Instruct your gymnast to stand with their back to the octagon.
Next, have them place their hands on the floor and then one shin on the octagon at a time.
Your gymnast should now be on their hands with their shins on the octagon.
Your gymnast's legs, hips, and chest should be off the floor at this time.
Next, instruct your gymnast to start with their body and legs straight.
Once your gymnast is completely straight with their shins on the octagon, instruct them to squeeze their buttocks.
Once they have their buttocks squeezed instruct your gymnast to pull their belly button in, just as if they were lifting their belly button off the floor in the **Belly Button Lift**. (P. 31)
You should see the lower portion of your gymnast's back elongate into the correct position for a handstand.
Once your gymnast squeezes their buttocks and pulls their belly button in they should begin to feel and perform the correct shape in their lower body for a handstand.
Your gymnast's buttocks should be tucked under once their belly button is pulled in.
Your gymnast has just performed the "pelvic tilt" and now will be expected to hold the pelvic tilt shape while in motion.
Once in the correct shape, instruct your gymnast to roll the octagon forward and back, keeping that rounded shape.
They should rock from their ankles to their knees, not allowing their knee caps or thighs to touch octagon.
Make sure your gymnast keeps their hands in one place while rocking forward and back.

# Gymnastics Drills and Conditioning
## For the Handstand

Instruct your gymnast to only rock as far forward as they comfortably can.
It is imperative your gymnast keep the their belly button in and buttocks squeezed while rocking forard and back.
Be sure your gymnast's head remains neutral and their legs remain straight throughout the exercise.

Have your gymnast relax and then repeat this drill several times. Make sure they start straight and then form the correct shape with their lower body before they begin to rock forward and back.

Once your gymnast has learned how to squeeze their buttocks and then pull their belly button in without changing anything else, ask them to push down on the floor (shrug) and pull in their chest so the portion of their back between their shoulder blades becomes rounded and more closely forms the shape necessary for a good handstand. (P. 47) Now instruct your gymnast perform the rock with their shoulders in this position, the shrug.

You can have your gymnast perfrom this drill on octagons of different heights for a change in shoulder and abdominal conditoning.

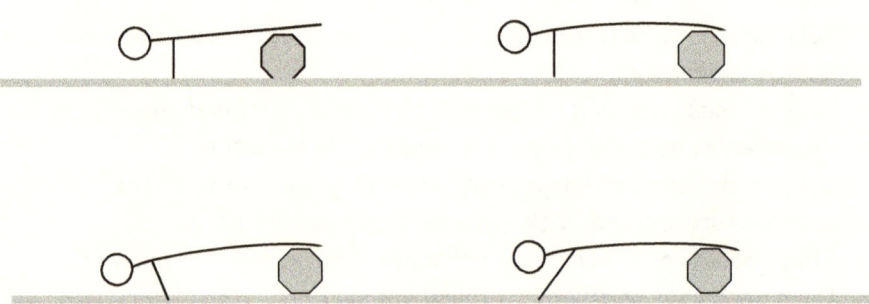

## Abdominal Control

**Octagon Tuck**
This is an abdominal conditioning and shape drill.
Have your gymnast stand in front of an octagon or barrel type mat.
Instruct your gymnast to stand with their back to the octagon.
Next, have them place their hands on the floor and then one foot and shin on the octagon at a time.
Your gymnast should now be on their hands with their shins on the octagon.
Have them start with their upper shins, the part closer to their knees, on the octagon rather than the part of their shins that is closer to their feet.
Your gymnast's legs, hips, and chest should be off the floor at this time.
Next, instruct your gymnast to start with their body and legs straight.
Once your gymnast is completely straight with their shins on the octagon, instruct them to squeeze their buttocks.
Once they have their buttocks squeezed instruct your gymnast to pull their belly button in, just as if they were lifting their belly button off the floor in the **Belly Button Lift**. (P. 31)
You should see the lower portion of your gymnast's back elongate into the correct position for a handstand.
Next, instruct your gymnast to push down on the floor (shrug) to form a rounded upper back. The portion of their back between their shoulder blades should be pushed up towards the ceiling which more closely forms the shape necessary for a good handstand. (P. 47)
Once your gymnast squeezes their buttocks and pulls their belly button in they should begin to feel and perform the correct shape in their lower body for a handstand.
Your gymnast's buttocks should be tucked under once their belly button is pulled in.
Your gymnast has just performed the "pelvic tilt" and now will be expected to hold the pelvic tilt shape while in motion.
Once in the correct shape, instruct your gymnast to slowly tuck their knees in toward their chest, keeping that rounded shape.

# Gymnastics Drills and Conditioning
# For the Handstand

Next, instruct your gymnast to keep the rounded shape and straighten their knees to open their hips again. They will return to the starting position, but keep the elongated lower back. Make sure your gymnast keeps their hands in one place while tucking in and opening back up.

Have your gymnast relax and then repeat this drill several times. Make sure they start straight and then form the correct shape with their lower body before they begin to tuck and open.

Your gymnast will first squeeze their buttocks, then pull in their belly button, then push down on the floor (shrug) and pull in their chest so they can better understand the shape of the proper handstand before they tuck and open.

You can have your gymnast perform this drill on octagons of different heights for a change in abdominal and shoulder conditoning.

## Shape and Shoulder Control

Now we'll focus on body shape, shoulder position, and strength. Many gymnasts are very well capable of standing on their hands, but many are still unaware of the fact that their shoulders must be free of angles and fully stretched. It can take a great deal of time for a gymnast to master the shoulder positions of the handstand. Here are some helpful drills involving the shoulder movements and positions necessary for a good handstand.

**Rounded Push up Position**
We will still be working with the correct pelvic tilt position.
Have your gymnast lie on their stomach, face down.
Use the floor exercise area or a firm mat.
Once your gymnast is on the floor, have them place their hands up by their armpits, so they can push up to a support, a push up position. Your gymnast's legs, hips, and chest all come up off the floor once they are in the push up position.
Instruct your gymnast to point their feet rather than keeping them flexed with the ball of their feet on the floor. Keeping their feet pointed puts more of a demand on your gymnast's abdominal muscles.
Next, instruct your gymnast to start with their body straight, but not sagging or arched.
Once your gymnast is completely straight, instruct them to squeeze their buttocks.
Once in the push up position with their buttocks squeezed, instruct your gymnast to pull their belly button in just as if they were lifting their belly button off the floor in the **Belly Button Lift**. (P. 31)
You should see the lower portion of your gymnast's back elongate into the correct position for a handstand.
Once your gymnast squeezes their buttocks and then pulls in their belly button they will have performed the "pelvic tilt" on their hands.

# Gymnastics Drills and Conditioning
## For the Handstand

Once your gymnast has formed the correct shape with their lower body, instruct them to push down on the floor and pull in their chest simultaneously.

The portion of your gymnast's back between the shoulder blades should rise toward the ceiling. Your gymnast has just performed a "**shoulder shrug**" in the push up position!

It often helps if you touch the portion of your gymnast's back between their shoulder blades and then ask them to push up on your hand to form the rounded position.

Be sure your gymnast's head remains neutral throughout the exercise.

Be sure your gymnast's legs remain straight and feet remain pointed throughout the exercise.

Once your gymnast knows how to push their upper back toward the ceiling and pull in their chest they should repeat the shrug motion several times.

Make sure your gymnast starts straight, performs the pelvic tilt, and then shrugs. Instruct your gymnast to keep the correct shape as they shrug several times before resting.

The illustration for this exercise is very general.

## Shape and Shoulder Control

**Rainbow Shrug**
We will be working with the correct pelvic tilt position.
Have your gymnast lie on their stomach, face down.
Use the floor exercise area or a firm mat.
Once your gymnast is on the floor, have them place their hands up by their armpits, so they can push up to a support, a push up position. Your gymnast's legs, hips, and chest all come up off the floor once they are in the push up position.
Instruct your gymnast to point their feet rather than keeping them flexed with the ball of their feet on the floor. Keeping their feet pointed puts more of a demand on your gymnast's abdominal muscles.
Next, instruct your gymnast to start with their body straight, but not sagging or arched.
Once your gymnast is completely straight, instruct them to walk their hands out enough so that their arms are nearly touching their ears. It will be a very long hand support position.
Once your gymnast is long and straight, instruct them to squeeze their buttocks.
Once in the very long hand support position with their buttocks squeezed, instruct your gymnast to pull their belly button in just as if they were lifting their belly button off the floor in the **Belly Button Lift**. (P. 31)
You should see the lower portion of your gymnast's back elongate into the correct position for a handstand.
Once your gymnast squeezes their buttocks and then pulls in their belly button they will have performed the "pelvic tilt" on their hands.
After your gymnast has formed the correct shape with their lower body, instruct them to push down on the floor and pull in their chest simultaneously.
The portion of your gymnast's back between their shoulder blades should rise toward the ceiling. Your gymnast has just performed a **Shoulder Shrug** in the rainbow position! This shape is called a Rainbow because it looks like a long rainbow.
Once you can see the rainbow shape, instruct your gymnast to keep their shoulders slightly higher than their buttocks.

## Gymnastics Drills and Conditioning
## For the Handstand

To help teach the shoulder shrug, touch the portion of your gymnast's back that is between their shoulder blades and ask them to push up on your hand to form the rounded position.
Be sure your gymnast's head remains neutral throughout the exercise.
Be sure your gymnast's legs remain straight throughout the exercise.
As your gymnast stretches to the longer rainbow position the demand on their abdominal muscles will increase dramatically.

Have your gymnast relax and then repeat this drill several times. Make sure they start straight, walk their hands out, perform the pelvic tilt, and then shrug. Instruct your gymnast to keep the correct shape as they shrug several times before resting.

The illustration for this drill is very general.

Shape and Shoulder Control

**Elevated Rainbow Shrug**
We will be working with the correct pelvic tilt position.
Have your gymnast lie on their stomach, face down.
Use the floor exercise area or a firm mat.
Place a folded panel mat near their feet so that your gymnast can place their (pointed) feet on the mat which is 8-12 inches high.
Instruct your gymnast to place the top portion of their feet and ankles on the mat. They can place part of their shin on the mat as well if it is more comfortable.
Once your gymnast is on the floor with their feet on the mat, have them place their hands up by their armpits, so they can push up to a support, a push up position. Your gymnast's legs, hips, and chest all come up off the floor for the elevated push up position.
Next, instruct your gymnast to start with their body straight, but not sagging or arched.
Once your gymnast is completely straight, instruct them to walk their hands out enough so that their arms are nearly touching their ears. It will be a very long hand support position.
Once your gymnast is completely straight with their arms close to their ears, instruct them to squeeze their buttocks.
Once in the hand support position with their buttocks squeezed, instruct your gymnast to pull their belly button in just as if they were lifting their belly button off the floor in the **Belly Button Lift.** (P. 31)
You should see the lower portion of your gymnast's back elongate into the correct position for a handstand.
Once your gymnast squeezes their buttocks and then pulls in their belly button they will have performed the "pelvic tilt" on their hands with their feet elevated.
Once your gymnast has formed the correct shape with their lower body, instruct them to push down on the floor and pull in their chest simultaneously.
The portion of your gymnast's back between the shoulder blades should rise toward the ceiling. Your gymnast has just performed a "shoulder shrug" in the rainbow position! This shape is called a rainbow because it looks like a long rainbow.

# Gymnastics Drills and Conditioning
## For the Handstand

To help teach the shrug touch the portion of your gymnast's back that is between their shoulder blades and ask them to push up on your hand to form the rounded position.

Once your gymnast knows how to push their upper back toward the ceiling they should repeat the rainbow shrug (push) several times.

Be sure your gymnast's head remains neutral and legs remain straight throughout the exercise.

Have your gymnast relax and then repeat this drill several times. Make sure they start straight, walk their hands out, perform the pelvic tilt, and then shrug. Instruct your gymnast to keep the correct shape as they shrug several times before resting.

The illustration for this drill is very general.

Shape and Shoulder Control

**Second Elevated Rainbow Shrug**
We will still be working with the correct pelvic tilt position. Place a spotting block which is 24 to 32 inches high (or two - three panel mats) on the floor so that your gymnast can place their feet on the block for this exercise.
Instruct your gymnast to stand with their back to the block. Next, have them place their hands on the floor and then one (pointed) foot on the block. Once they have one foot on the block, your gymnast can then place their other foot on the block.
Your gymnast can place part of their shin on the block as well if it is more comfortable for them.
Now your gymnast should be in a push support with their feet on the block.
Your gymnast's legs, hips, and chest all remain off the floor for the elevated push up position.
Next, instruct your gymnast to start with their body straight, but not sagging or arched.
Once your gymnast is completely straight, instruct them to walk their hands out enough so that their arms are nearly touching their ears. It will be a very long hand support position.
Once your gymnast is completely straight, instruct them to squeeze their buttocks.
Once in the elevated hand support position with their arms close to their ears and buttocks squeezed, instruct your gymnast to pull their belly button in just as if they were lifting their belly button off the floor in the **Belly Button Lift**. (P. 31)
You should see the lower portion of your gymnast's back elongate into the correct position for a handstand.
Once your gymnast squeezes their buttocks and then pulls in their belly button they will have performed the "pelvic tilt" on their hands and in the rainbow position.
Once your gymnast has formed the correct shape with their lower body, instruct them to push down on the floor and pull in their chest simultaneously.
The portion of your gymnast's back between the shoulder blades should rise toward the ceiling. Your gymnast has just performed a

# Gymnastics Drills and Conditioning
## For the Handstand

"shoulder shrug" in the rainbow position! This shape is called a rainbow because it looks like a long rainbow.

To help teach the shrug touch the portion of your gymnast's back that is between their shoulder blades and ask them to push up on your hand to form the rounded position.

Once your gymnast knows how to push their upper back toward the ceiling they should repeat the rainbow shrug (push) several times.

Be sure your gymnast's head remains neutral and legs remain straight throughout the exercise.

Have your gymnast relax and then repeat the drill several times. Make sure they start straight, walk their hands out, perform the pelvic tilt, pull in their belly button, and then shrug. Instruct your gymnast to keep the correct shape as they shrug several times before resting.

The illustration for this drill is very general.

## Shape and Shoulder Control

**Third Elevated Rainbow Shrug**
We will be working with the correct pelvic tilt position.
Place a spotting block which is 36-48 inches high (or three - four panel mats) on the floor so that your gymnast can place their feet on the block for this exercise. If you are using a spotting block flip it so it is near the recommended height.
A balance beam can also be used, but it will not feel as comfortable on your gymnast's feet.
Instruct your gymnast to stand with their back to the block.
Next, have them place their hands on the floor and then one foot on the block. Once they have one foot on the block, your gymnast can then place their other foot on the block.
Your gymnast can also place part of their shin on the block if it is more comfortable for them.
Now your gymnast should be in a push up support with their feet on the block.
Your gymnast's legs, hips, and chest all remain off the floor for the elevated push up position.
Next, instruct your gymnast to start with their body straight, but not sagging or arched.
Once your gymnast is completely straight, instruct them to walk their hands out enough so that their arms are nearly touching their ears. It will be a very long hand support position.
Once your gymnast is completely straight, instruct them to squeeze their buttocks.
Once in the high elevated hand support position with their buttocks squeezed and arms close to their ears, instruct your gymnast to pull their belly button in just as if they were lifting their belly button off the floor in the **Belly Button Lift**. (P. 31)
You should see the lower portion of your gymnast's back elongate into the correct position for a handstand.
Once your gymnast squeezes their buttocks and then pulls in their belly button they will have performed the "pelvic tilt" in the elevated hand support position.
Once your gymnast has formed the correct shape with their lower body, instruct them to push down on the floor and pull in

# Gymnastics Drills and Conditioning
## For the Handstand

their chest simultaneously. The portion of your gymnast's back between their shoulder blades should rise toward the ceiling. Your gymnast's shoulders should get closer to their ears with each shrug.

Your gymnast has just performed a "shoulder shrug" in the very high elevated push up position! This shape is called a rainbow because it looks like a long rainbow.

To help teach the shrug touch the portion of this drill touch the part of your gymnast's back that is between their shoulder blades and ask them to push up on your hand to form the rounded position.

Be sure your gymnast's head remains neutral and legs remain straight throughout this exercise.

Have your gymnast relax and then repeat the drill several times. Make sure they start straight, walk their hands out, perform the pelvic tilt, pull in their belly button, and then shrug. Instruct your gymnast to keep the correct shape as they shrug several times before resting.

With each increase in elevation there is an increase in demand on upper body muscles because more weight is being supported by the upper body rather than it being more evenly distributed as in a very low elevation.

The illustration for this drill is very general.

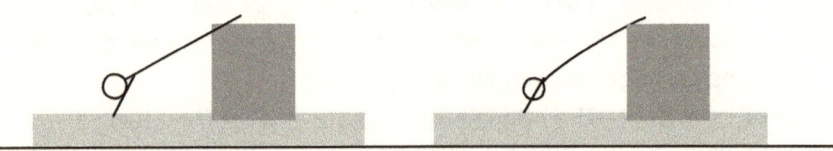

# Handstand Production

**Wall Climb**
This is for shoulder conditioning, shape, and remaining tight in motion.
Please spot your gymnast for these drills.
Have your gymnast stand with their back close to a padded wall.
Make sure the padding or mat will not fall on your gymnast.
Next, instruct your gymnast to place their hands on the floor\mat approximately 2 feet from wall.
Once their hands are on the floor, instruct your gymnast to place one foot on the wall at a time. Instruct your gymnast to pull in their belly button and squeeze their buttocks.
If your gymnast is comfortable in that position, they are ready to progress to the next step.

**Once your gymnast is strong enough in that position…**
Have your gymnast come down and rest before you expect them to move to the next step in the **Wall Progressions**.
Have your gymnast stand with their back close to padded wall.
Next, instruct them to place their hands on floor\mat approximately 2 feet from wall.
Have them start further from the wall as they advance.
Once their hands are on the floor, instruct your gymnast to place one foot on the wall at a time.
Next, instruct your gymnast to pull in their belly button and squeeze their buttocks.
Once your gymnast is stable and tight, instruct them to move one hand closer to the wall.
Once they are able to move one hand closer to the wall, instruct your gymnast to move the other hand closer to the wall and allow their feet to slide up the wall.
Instruct your gymnast to simultaneously walk their hands in towards wall and their feet up wall towards the ceiling until their forehead touches the wall and their shoulders touch their ears.

Copyright © Goeller 2005

# Gymnastics Drills and Conditioning For the Handstand

Make sure your gymnast remains tight, keeping their buttocks squeezed and belly button in, throughout this drill.

Once your gymnast reaches the handstand instruct them to shrug by pushing down on the floor until their ears reach their shoulders.

To help teach the shrug in the handstand position rest your hand on top of your gymnast's toes and ask them to push up on your hand with their toes.

Make sure you spot your gymnast while they are performing this drill.

Keeping their arms straight, instruct your gymnast to either walk back out, remaining very tight or allow them to roll out.

If you ask your gymnast to forward roll out of the handstand, remind your gymnast to keep their arms straight and tuck their head in as they are rolling.

This exercise will help strengthen your gymnast's upper body, especially their shoulders as well as their abdominal muscles.

Have your gymnast relax and then repeat this drill a few times. This drill puts a large amount of pressure on a gymnast's wrists. Your gymnast should stop when their wrists feel uncomfortable.

**Advanced Wall Climb Work**
Once your gymnast has mastered the **Wall Climb**, have them see if they can connect a few **Wall Climbs** without stopping. They will climb, walk back out, and then climb again.
This drill can help tremendously with Cast Handstand and Clear Hip work on uneven bars!

**Advanced Wall Climb Work**
Once your gymnast has mastered the **Wall Climb,** have them perform several shrugs while in the handstand without stopping before they walk back out or roll out.
This drill can help tremendously with Cast Handstand and Clear Hip work on uneven bars!

**Very Advanced Wall Climb Work for Competitive Gymnasts**

## Handstand Production

Once your gymnast has mastered the **Wall Climb**, have them perform a half pirouette and then return to the starting position by pirouetting back.
This drill can help tremendously with Handstand work on uneven bars, especially pirouettes!

**Take precautions**...The mat must be secured against wall and the inexperienced gymnast must be spotted closely in order to prevent falling into an arched position against wall. Instruct your gymnast to come down as soon as they are fatigued. Be sure to warn your gymnast not to fall into an arched position against the wall.

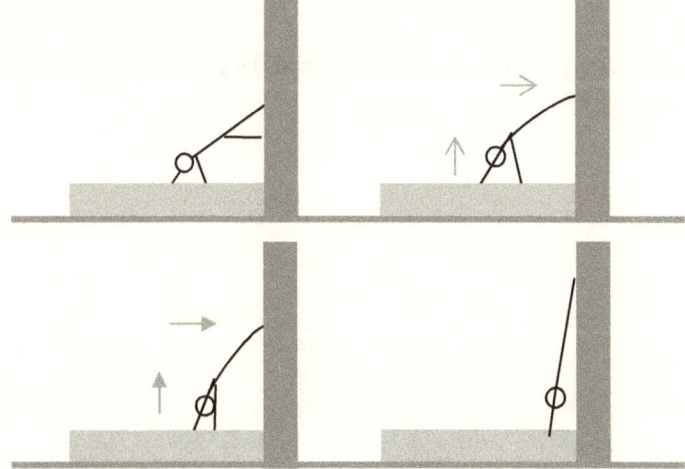

You can have your gymnast walk back out after they perform the **Wall Climb**.

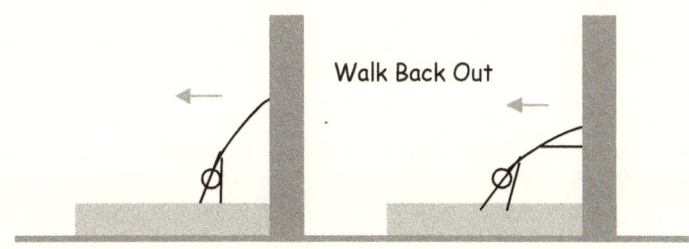

# Gymnastics Drills and Conditioning
## For the Handstand

You can have your gymnast roll out after then perform the Wall Climb

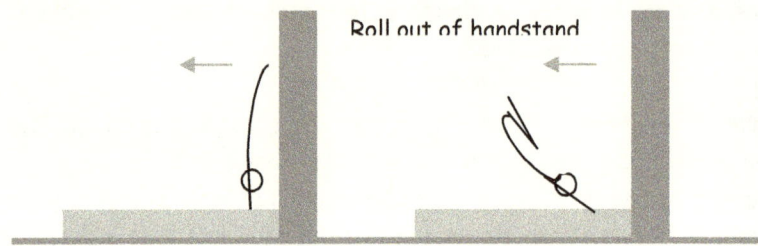

Roll out of handstand

You can have your very advanced gymnasts pirouette after they perform the **Wall Climb**.

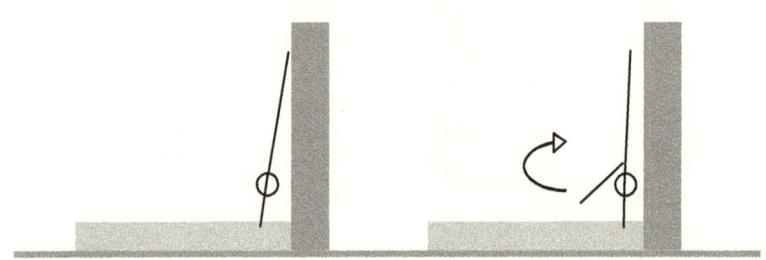

# Handstand Production

By this point your gymnast may be able to kick to a handstand on their own and remain tight if you help them balance. If they have performed all of the drills before this point along with participating in your regular gymnastics curriculum your gymnast should be able to move onto the next set of drills which require the complete handstand.

## Handstand Shrug

Be ready to spot your gymnast for this handstand.
Inform your gymnast they will be required to remain in the handstand for a substantial amount of time, long enough to focus on shape and body tightness.
Give your gymnast full instructions before requiring them to kick to the handstand.
Instruct your gymnast to kick to a handstand.
Once your gymnast is in the handstand ask them to pull their belly button in as if they are performing the **Belly Button Lift**.
Next instruct them to squeeze their buttocks and watch for their lower back to remain in the elongated or pelvic tilt position.
If the correct position is not reached quickly, ask your gymnast to lie on the floor and perform the **Belly Button Lift** as a friendly reminder of the correct shape. (P. 31)
Once your gymnast has been reminded of the **Belly Button Lift** ask them to kick to the handstand again and perform the first two tasks, the **Belly Button Lift** and the **Buttocks Squeeze**.
Next have them shrug their shoulders. Remind them to pull in their chest.
Once your gymnast has demonstrated the correct shape ask them to flex their feet.
After your gymnast has flexed their feet place your hand on your gymnast's heels and instruct them to push up on your hand.
If your gymnast is able to successfully push up on your hand you should see their ears rise up to their shoulders.
There should be no space between your gymnast's ears and shoulders if they have completely and correctly performed the shrug.

# Gymnastics Drills and Conditioning
## For the Handstand

Inform your gymnast that the shrug should be performed in every handstand.

The illustration is very general.

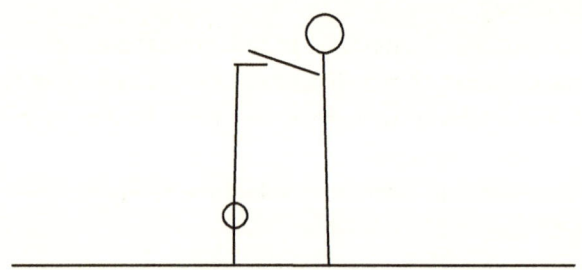

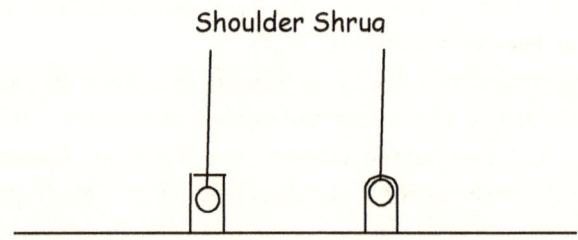

Shoulder Shrug

## Handstand Production

**Handstand Shrug – Feet Together**
Be ready to spot your gymnast for this handstand.
Inform your gymnast they will be required to remain in the handstand for a substantial amount of time, long enough to focus on shape and body tightness.
Give your gymnast full instructions before requiring them to kick to the handstand.
Instruct your gymnast to kick to a handstand.
Once in the handstand ask them to pull their belly button in as if they are performing the **Belly Button Lift**. (P. 31)
Next instruct them to squeeze their buttocks and watch for their lower back to remain in the elongated or pelvic tilt position.
If the correct position is not reached quickly, ask your gymnast to lie on the floor and perform the **Belly Button Lift** with the **Buttocks Squeeze** as a friendly reminder of the correct shape.
Once your gymnast has been reminded of the **Belly Button Lift** ask them to kick to the handstand again and perform the first two tasks, the **Belly Button Lift** and the **Buttocks Squeeze**.
Next have your gymnast shrug their shoulders. Remind them to pull in their chest if necessary.
Once your gymnast has demonstrated the correct shape inform them they must keep their feet together.
After your gymnast has been instructed to keep their feet together, gently try to separate your gymnast's feet.
Attempt to pull them toward a straddle and then toward a split with either foot in front.
Only try to separate your gymnast's feet a few inches. If you are successful with separating your gymnast's feet at all, remind your gymnast to squeeze their thighs together in order to help keep their feet together.
Have your gymnast step down from the handstand and lay on the floor on either their stomach or back.
Once your gymnast is on the floor, instruct them to keep their feet together by squeezing their thighs together.
After your gymnast has been instructed to keep their feet together, try to separate your gymnast's feet a few inches.

# Gymnastics Drills and Conditioning
## For the Handstand

If your gymnast was able to keep their feet together while on the floor, allow them to attempt the drill in the handstand again. Ask your gymnast to kick up to a handstand.

Once they are in a tight handstand make sure they are in the correct shape, pelvic tilt, buttocks squeezed, shoulders stretched into a shrug, and chest in, try to separate your gymnast's feet a few inches.

Many gymnast's are successful the second time with this drill. Remember, your gymnast must remain in the very stretched and straight handstand the entire time.

The illustration for this drill is very general.

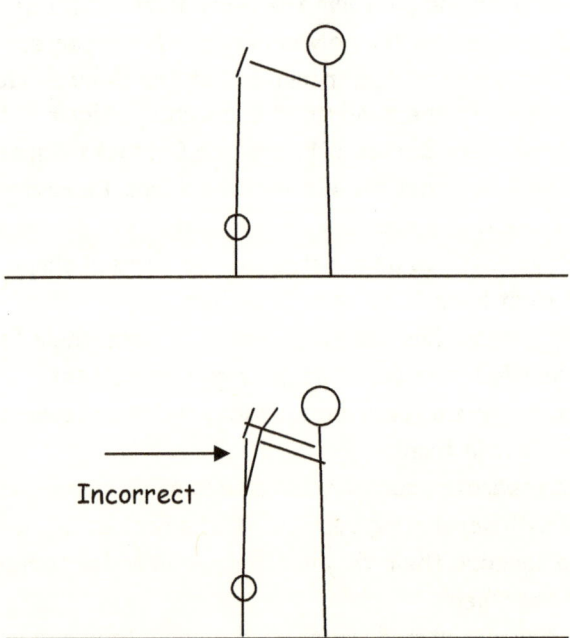

Incorrect

## Handstand Production

**Handstand - Tight and Stable**
**Advanced Handstand Work**
Be ready to spot your gymnast for this handstand.
Inform your gymnast they will be required to remain in the handstand for a substantial amount of time, long enough to focus on shape and body tightness.
Give your gymnast full instructions before requiring them to kick to the handstand.
Instruct your gymnast to kick to a handstand.
Once your gymnast is in the handstand ask them to pull their belly button in as if they are performing the **Belly Button Lift**.
Next instruct them to squeeze their buttocks and watch for their lower back to remain in the elongated or pelvic tilt position.
If the correct position is not reached quickly, ask your gymnast to lie on the floor and perform the **Belly Button Lift** as a friendly reminder of the correct shape. (P. 31)
Once your gymnast has been reminded of the **Belly Button Lift** ask them to kick to the handstand again and perform the first two tasks, the **Belly Button Lift** and the **Buttocks Squeeze**.
Next have your gymnast shrug their shoulders. Remind them to pull in their chest if necessary.
Once your gymnast has demonstrated the correct shape ask them to flex their feet.
After your gymnast has flexed their feet place your hand on their heels and instruct them to push up on your hand.
If your gymnast is able to successfully push up on your hand you should see their ears rise up to their shoulders.
Once in the completely stretched and tight handstand position, your gymnast should be ready for light resistance.
Remind your gymnast you are about to press down on their heels.
Gently press down on your gymnast's heels to check to see if they have kept the correct shape and remained tight.
Be ready to spot your gymnast, if your press down too hard they will fall.

Remember, we are testing for the pelvic tilt, buttocks squeeze, and the shoulder shrug.

# Gymnastics Drills and Conditioning
## For the Handstand

There should be no space between your gymnast's ears and shoulders if they have completely and correctly performed the shrug.

Instruct your gymnast to remain tight and not allow their back to arch, hips to flex, arms to bend, or shoulders to sink.

As you are pressing your gymnast's heels you must keep safety in mind and constantly remind them to keep their belly in, their buttocks squeezed, and their shoulders shrugged.

Remember to instruct your gymnast to tell you if they are fatigued.

**Take precautions...**
Do not press down hard because it can cause your gymnast to collapse or be injured. Only perform this tightness check if your gymnast is physically and mentally able to resist light pressure.

When you press down on your gymnast in the handstand position from their heels you are greatly increasing the demand on your gymnast's entire body, especially their upper body. Allow your gymnast to rest or discontinue this handstand work if their wrists or anything else become uncomfortable, fatigued, or sore.

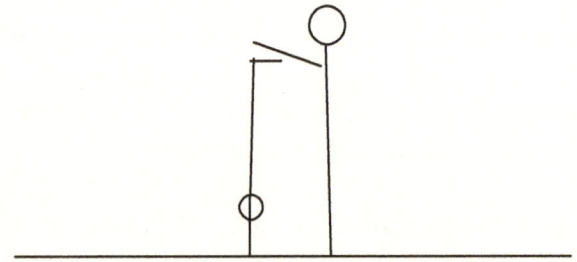

# Handstand Production

**Handstand, Tuck, Open**
Be ready to spot your gymnast for this drill.
Inform your gymnast they will be required to remain in the handstand for a substantial amount of time, long enough to focus on shape and body tightness.
Give your gymnast full instructions before requiring them to kick to the handstand.
Instruct your gymnast to kick to a handstand.
Once your gymnast is in the handstand ask them to pull their belly button in as if they are performing the **Belly Button Lift**.
Next instruct them to squeeze their buttocks and watch for their lower back to remain in the elongated or pelvic tilt position.
If the correct position is not reached quickly, ask your gymnast to lie on the floor and perform the **Belly Button Lift** as a friendly reminder of the correct shape. (P. 31)
Once your gymnast has been reminded of the **Belly Button Lift** ask them to kick to the handstand again and perform the first two tasks, the **Belly Button Lift** and the **Buttocks Squeeze**.
Next have them shrug their shoulders. Remind your gymnast to pull in their chest if necessary.
Make sure you test their shoulder shrug and tightness by gently pressing down on your gymnast's heels prior to performing the next step.
Once your gymnast has demonstrated the correct stretch and shape instruct them to slowly bring their knees down toward their chest but to keep the correct shoulder stretch and position.
Make sure your gymnast leads the movement with their knees rather than bringing their heels to their buttocks. If they bring their heels to their buttocks they may not maintain the correct pelvic tilt shape.
Your gymnast's shins must remain perpendicular to the floor the entire time, including during the movement down and up.
Inform your gymnast that they must not allow their shoulders to sink or form an angle. Even at the bottom of the tuck your gymnast's shoulders should not have an angle.

# Gymnastics Drills and Conditioning
## For the Handstand

Once your gymnast has reached the tuck position, instruct them to begin to open their knees by raising their feet to the ceiling. They should open their hips and knees at the same rate of speed. Instruct your gymnast to continue to keep their shoulders stretched, their belly button in, and their buttocks under as they open their hips and knees.

The focus is on attaining and then keeping the correct shape before, during, and after the tuck movement.

Many gymnasts need to attempt this skill several times before they are able to keep the rounded back upon opening from the tuck.

## Handstand Production

**Wall Handstand Tuck Open**
Have your gymnast stand with their back close to a padded wall.
Make sure the padding\mat will not fall on your gymnast.
Next, instruct your gymnast to place their hands on the floor\mat approximately 1-2 feet from wall.
Once their hands are on the floor, instruct your gymnast to place one foot on the wall at a time.
If your gymnast is comfortable in that position, they are ready to progress to the next step.
Be ready to spot your gymnast for this drill.
Inform your gymnast they will be required to remain in the handstand for a substantial amount of time, long enough to focus on shape.
Give your gymnast full instructions before requiring them to climb to the handstand.
Instruct your gymnast to climb to a handstand, as they did in the Wall Climb, but as close to the wall.
Your gymnast will need enough space for their shins to slide down the wall.
Once your gymnast is in the handstand ask them to pull their belly button in as if they are performing the **Belly Button Lift**.
Next instruct them to squeeze their buttocks and watch for their lower back to remain in the elongated or pelvic tilt position.
If the correct position is not reached quickly, ask your gymnast to lie on the floor and perform the **Belly Button Lift** as a friendly reminder of the correct shape. (P. 31)
Once your gymnast has been reminded of the **Belly Button Lift** ask them to climb to the handstand again and perform the first two tasks, the **Belly Button Lift** and the **Buttocks Squeeze**.
Next have your gymnast shrug their shoulders. Remind your gymnast to pull in their chest if necessary.
Make sure you test their shoulder shrug and tightness by gently pressing down on your gymnast's heels prior to performing the next step.
Once your gymnast has demonstrated the correct stretch and shape instruct them to slowly bring their knees down toward

# Gymnastics Drills and Conditioning
## For the Handstand

their chest but to keep the correct shoulder stretch and position.

It may be easier for your gymnast to understand the correct motion if you instruct them to slide their shins and toes down the wall until their knees come close to their chest.

Make sure your gymnast leads the movement with their knees rather than bringing their heels to their buttocks. If they bring their heels to their buttocks they may not maintain the correct pelvic tilt shape and they may lose their balance.

Your gymnast's shins must remain perpendicular to the floor the entire time, including during the movement down and up.

Inform your gymnast that they must not allow their shoulders to sink or form an angle. Even at the bottom of the tuck your gymnast's shoulders should not have an angle.

Once your gymnast has reached the tuck position, instruct them to begin to open their knees by raising their feet toward the ceiling or sliding their shins back up the wall. They should open their hips and knees at the same rate of speed.

Instruct your gymnast to continue to keep their shoulders stretched, their belly button in, and their buttocks under as they open their hips and knees.

The focus is on attaining and then keeping the correct shape, especially in the lower back, during and after movement.

Many gymnasts need to attempt this skill several times before they are able to keep the rounded back upon opening from the tuck.

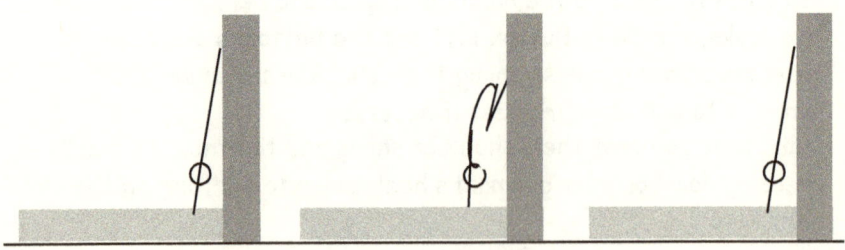

# Shape in Motion

**Rainbow to Handstand to Rainbow**
This is a body tightness drill.
Have your gymnast lie on their stomach, face down.
Use the floor exercise area or a firm mat.
Once your gymnast is on the floor, have them place their hands up by their armpits, so they can push up to a support, a push up position. Your gymnast's legs, hips, and chest all come up off the floor once they are in the push up position.
Instruct your gymnast to point their feet rather than keeping them flexed with the ball of their feet on the floor. Keeping their feet pointed puts more of a demand on your gymnast's abdominal muscles.
Next, instruct your gymnast to start with their body straight, but not sagging or arched.
Once your gymnast is completely straight, instruct them to walk their hands out enough so that their arms are nearly touching their ears. It will be a very long hand support position.
Once your gymnast is long and straight, instruct them to squeeze their buttocks.
Once in the very long hand support position with their buttocks squeezed, instruct your gymnast to pull their belly button in just as if they were lifting their belly button off the floor in the **Belly Button Lift**. (P. 31)
You should see the lower portion of your gymnast's back elongate into the correct position for a handstand.
Once your gymnast squeezes their buttocks and then pulls in their belly button they will have performed the "pelvic tilt" on their hands and in the rainbow position.
After your gymnast has formed the correct shape with their lower body, instruct them to push down on the floor and pull in their chest simultaneously.
The portion of your gymnast's back between the shoulder blades should rise toward the ceiling. Your gymnast has just performed a **"shoulder shrug"** in the rainbow position! This shape is called a

# Gymnastics Drills and Conditioning
# For the Handstand

rainbow because it looks like a long rainbow. Instruct your gymnast to keep their shoulders slightly higher than their buttocks.

To help teach the shrug touch the portion of your gymnast's back that is between their shoulder blades and ask them to push up on your hand to form the rounded position.

Be sure your gymnast's head remains neutral throughout the exercise.

Be sure your gymnast's legs remain straight throughout the exercise.

Next instruct your gymnast to hold that tight shape throughout the rest of the drill.

Once your gymnast is informed, start to lift their heels toward the ceiling.

You will actually need to lift your gymnast by their shins, not by their toes, thighs, belly, or hips.

Lift your gymnast's feet slowly because if they lose the shape you must lower them back to the rainbow position to correct the shape and then make another attempt at the **Rainbow to Handstand**.

Each time your gymnast performs the **Rainbow to Handstand** they must be returned to the Rainbow. It is just as important for your gymnast to keep the correct shape and remain tight on the way down as it was for them to keep the correct shape and remain tight on the way up.

When you are lifting your gymnast's shins toward the ceiling, gently shift their weight forward rather than pulling them away from their hands in order to prevent them from collapsing.

Once your gymnast is successful in completing the **Rainbow to Handstand** and then returning to the Rainbow have them perform shoulder shrugs in the handstand before you lower them back to the rainbow position.

Constantly remind your gymnast to keep the pelvic tilt, their buttocks squeezed, their chest in, and their shoulders in line throughout the entire drill.

Be sure your gymnast's head remains neutral throughout the exercise.

## Shape in Motion

Be sure your gymnast's legs remain straight and their feet remain pointed throughout the exercise.

Have your gymnast relax and then repeat this drill a few times. Make sure they start straight, perform the pelvic tilt, buttocks squeeze, and then shrug. Instruct your gymnast to keep the correct shape as they are lifted and lowered several times before resting.

This is a body tightness drill, not a planche drill.

As your gymnast stretches to the longer rainbow position the demand on their abdominal muscles will increase dramatically. The constant change in elevation causes a change in the demand on your gymnast's abdominal and upper body muscles. With each increase in elevation there is an increase in demand on upper body muscles because more weight is being supported by their upper body rather than it being more evenly distributed as in a very low or no elevation.

# Gymnastics Drills and Conditioning
## For the Handstand

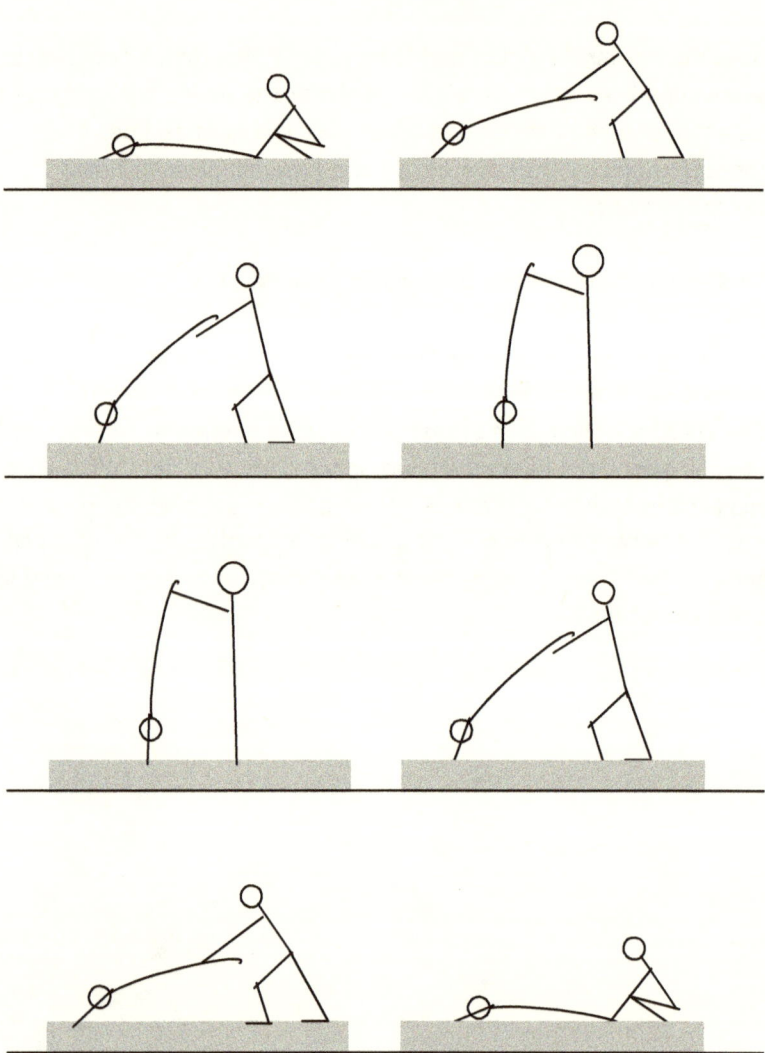

## Shape in Motion

**Planche - Forward and Back**
This is for body tightness and strength in the planche position. It is useful for the handstand on floor as well as the cast to handstand on uneven bars with more advanced gymnasts!
We'll be working with the correct pelvic tilt position as well.
Have your gymnast stand in front of a folded panel mat or a low balance beam (for the more advanced gymnasts) which should be about 6-8 inches high. A very stable floor bar can be used as well.
Once your gymnast is in front of the low beam, instruct them to place their hands on the beam. Your gymnast should be in a push up position. Your gymnast's legs, hips, and chest should all be off the floor once they are in the push up position with their hands on the low beam.
Next, instruct your gymnast to start with their body straight, but not sagging or arched.
Once your gymnast is straight, instruct them to squeeze their buttocks.
Once in the push up position with their buttocks squeezed, instruct your gymnast to pull their belly button in just as if they were lifting their belly button off the floor in the **Belly Button Lift**. (P. 31)
You should see the lower portion of your gymnast's back elongate into the correct position for a handstand.
Once your gymnast squeezes their buttocks and then pulls in their belly button they will have performed the "pelvic tilt" on their hands.
After your gymnast has formed the correct shape with their lower body, instruct them to push down on the low beam and pull in their chest simultaneously.
The portion of your gymnast's back between the shoulder blades should rise toward the ceiling. Your gymnast has just performed a **"shoulder shrug"** in the push up position with their upper body slightly elevated.
To help teach the shrug touch the portion of your gymnast's back that is between their shoulder blades and ask them to push up on your hand to form the rounded position.

# Gymnastics Drills and Conditioning
# For the Handstand

Be sure your gymnast's head remains neutral throughout the exercise.

Be sure your gymnast's legs remain straight throughout the exercise.

They are now ready to be spotted for this drill.

Next instruct your gymnast to hold that tight shape throughout the rest of the planche drill.

Once your gymnast is informed, **lift their feet approximately one foot off the floor.** Your gymnast's shoulders should still be directly above the low beam at this point.

You should actually lift your gymnast by their shins, not by their toes, thighs, belly, or hips.

Lift your gymnast's legs slowly because if they lose the shape you must lower them back to the **Rounded Push Up** position to correct the shape and then make another attempt at the **Rounded Push Up** position.

Once your gymnast is in the correct position with you holding their shins, slowly shift their weight forward a few inches so they are in a slight planche position and then return them to the starting position by gently pulling their weight back.

Once your gymnast understands the motion, instruct them to initiate and control the forward and return movement. At this point you should just hold the weight of your gymnast's shins without controlling the forward or backward movement.

Inform your gymnast not to planche too far forward until they are very comfortable so they do not collapse and land on the low beam.

You must also inform your gymnast not to push back too far until they are very comfortable so they do not collapse to the floor.

You can either spot as if you are holding a wheel barrel or you can stand on the side of your gymnast and spot.

Each time your gymnast rocks forward, they must rock back to the starting position to complete one full repetition of this drill.

It is just as important for your gymnast to keep the correct shape and remain tight on the rock back as it was for them to keep the correct shape and remain tight on the rock forward, the planche.

## Shape in Motion

Constantly remind your gymnast to keep the pelvic tilt, their buttocks squeezed, their chest in, and their arms straight (not locked in the elbows) throughout the entire drill.
Be sure your gymnast's head remains in line with their spine throughout the exercise.
Be sure your gymnast's legs remain straight throughout the exercise.

Have your gymnast relax and then repeat this drill a few times. Make sure they start straight, perform the pelvic tilt, buttocks squeeze, the shrug, and then the rock forward. Instruct your gymnast to keep the correct shape as they are lifted and then perform the planche drill.

This exercise can put tremendous pressure on your gymnast's wrists and shoulders. You should allow them to stop this drill when their wrists and shoulders become uncomfortable.

**Advanced Planche Work**
Once your gymnast is successful in completing the planche and return, you can have them perform shoulder shrugs in the planche position before they return to the starting position.

Once your gymnast has mastered this drill in the natural\over grip position, they can attempt this drill in an under grip position to help them prepare for front giant work on uneven bars.

With each rock forward there is change in demand on the upper body muscles. Your gymnast may eventually develop strength in a wider range of positions after performing this drill over the course of time.

# Gymnastics Drills and Conditioning
## For the Handstand

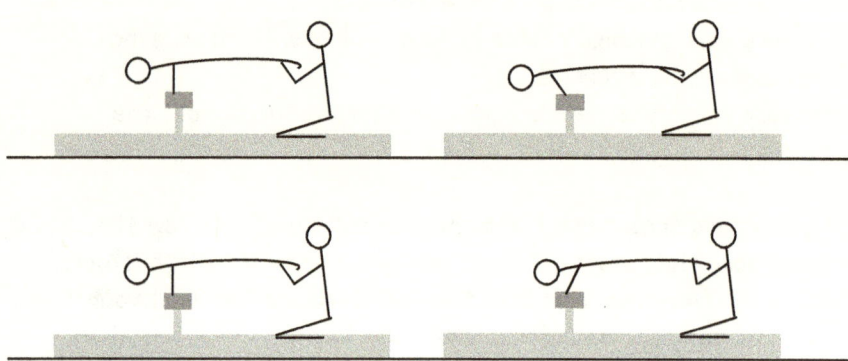

You can use either the wheel barrel method or stand beside your gymnast to spot.

Shape in Motion

**Planche - Handstand - Planche**
This drill is for body tightness and strength in the planche position. It is useful for the handstand on floor as well as the cast to handstand on uneven bars with more advanced gymnasts. You can use the floor exercise area or allow your gymnast to use the low beam, a panel mat, or a stable floor bar.

Have your gymnast stand in front of a folded panel mat or a low balance beam which should be about 6-8 inches high. Many gymnasts prefer using a panel mat or low beam because they can grasp the top and side of the beam as they would in a cartwheel. Once your gymnast is in front of the low beam, instruct them to place their hands on the beam. Your gymnast's body should be perpendicular to the low beam and they should be in a push up position. Your gymnast's legs, hips, and chest should all be off the floor with their hands on the low beam.

Next, instruct your gymnast to start with their body straight, not sagging or arched.

Once your gymnast is straight, instruct them to squeeze their buttocks.

Once in the push up position with their buttocks squeezed, instruct your gymnast to pull their belly button in just as if they were lifting their belly button off the floor in the **Belly Button Lift**. (P. 31)

You should see the lower portion of your gymnast's back elongate into the correct position for a handstand.

Once your gymnast squeezes their buttocks and then pulls in their belly button they will have performed the "pelvic tilt" in a push up position.

After your gymnast has formed the correct shape with their lower body, instruct them to push down on the low beam and pull in their chest simultaneously to form the **Rounded Push Up** position. (P. 47)

The portion of your gymnast's back between their shoulder blades should rise toward the ceiling. Your gymnast has just performed a "shoulder shrug" in the push up position with their upper body slightly elevated.

# Gymnastics Drills and Conditioning
## For the Handstand

To help teach the shrug touch the portion of your gymnast's back that is between their shoulder blades and ask them to push up on your hand to form the rounded position.

Your gymnast should now be ready for the **Planche-Handstand-Planche** drill.

Instruct your gymnast to hold that tight shape throughout the rest of the **Planche-Handstand-Planche** drill.

Once your gymnast is informed, lift their feet\ankles to a handstand position. Your gymnast's shoulders, hips, and ankles should be directly above their hands at this point.

It is often easier to lift gymnasts by their shins rather than their feet.

Remember to lift your gymnast's body to the handstand slowly because if they lose the shape you must lower them back to the **Rounded Push Up** position to correct the shape and then make another attempt at the tight handstand position.

Once your gymnast is in the correct handstand position with you holding their shins, slowly and gently lower your gymnast's shins 4-6 inches and help them shift their weight forward a few inches so they are in a slight planche position.

Next, return your gymnast back up to the handstand position by gently pulling their weight back up and instructing them to pull their head and shoulders back into alignment for the handstand position. You can help your gymnast return to the handstand by spotting with one hand at their shoulders and the other spotting their shins.

Once your gymnast understands the motion of the handstand to the slight planche and back to the handstand, instruct them to initiate and control the planche downward and forward and then have them initiate and control the return movement back up to the handstand.

Make sure you are spotting this drill carefully by helping your gymnast to balance and control the planche down and up.

Inform your gymnast not to planche too far forward until they are very comfortable.

Each time your gymnast lowers and rocks forward, they must return their shoulders back into the correct alignment for the

## Shape in Motion

handstand position in order to complete one full repetition of this drill.
It is just as important for your gymnast to keep the correct shape and remain tight on the return motion as it was for them to keep the correct shape and remain tight on the planche motion. Constantly remind your gymnast to keep the pelvic tilt, their buttocks squeezed, their chest in, and their arms straight (not locked in the elbows) throughout the entire drill.
Be sure your gymnast's legs remain straight throughout the exercise.

Have your gymnast relax and then repeat this drill a few times. Make sure they start straight, perform the pelvic tilt, buttocks squeeze, and the shrug before you lift them to the handstand. Instruct your gymnast to keep the correct shape as they are lifted and as they perform the planche drill.

This exercise puts tremendous pressure on your gymnast's wrists and upper body. You should allow them to stop performing this drill when their wrists and shoulders become uncomfortable. Inform your gymnast to communicate with you when they are fatigued. They should stop performing this drill for the day when they become fatigued or uncomfortable.

Once your gymnast has mastered this drill in the natural\over grip position, they can attempt this drill in an under grip position to help them prepare for front giant work on uneven bars.
This is a body tightness and planche drill.

The constant change in shoulder angle causes a change in the demand on your gymnast's upper body muscles. Your gymnast may eventually develop strength in a wider range of positions after performing this drill over the course of time. This drill can help tremendously with Cast Handstand and Clear Hip work on uneven bars.

# Gymnastics Drills and Conditioning For the Handstand

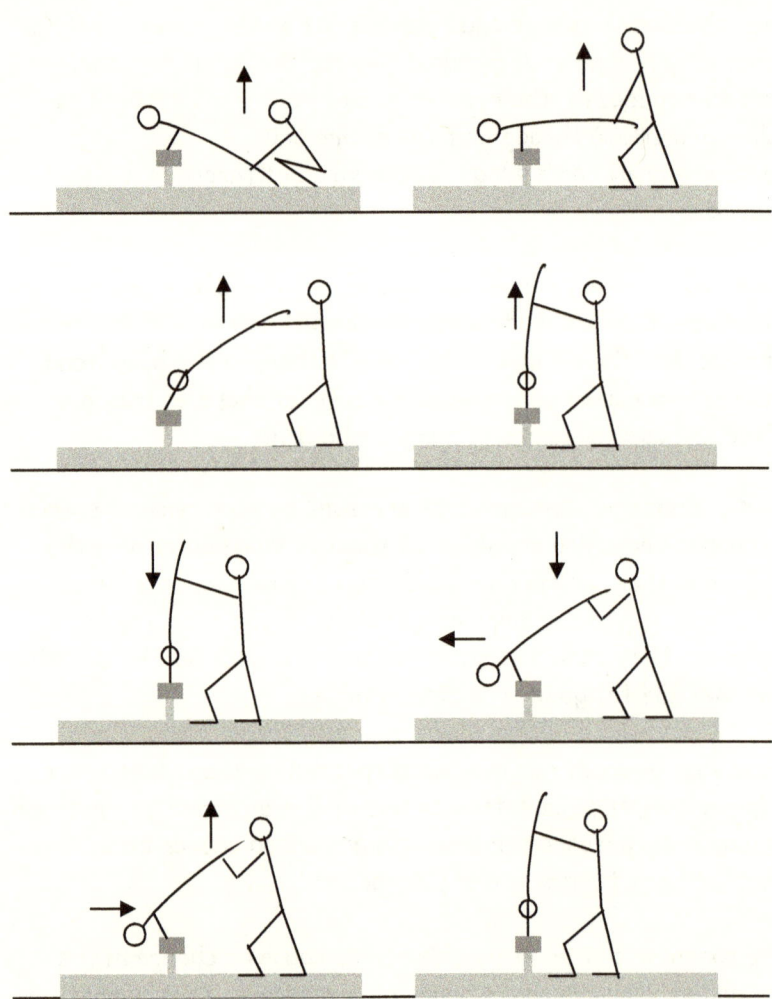

## Shape in Motion

**Planche - Virtual Handstand - Planche**

This is for body tightness and strength in the planche position. It is useful for the handstand on floor as well as the cast to handstand on uneven bars with more advanced gymnasts!

We'll be working with the correct pelvic tilt position as well. Place a spotting block which is 36-48 inches high (or three - four panel mats) on the floor so that your gymnast can place their feet on the block and hands on the floor exercise area or opened mat for this drill.

A medium to high balance beam can also be used, but it will not feel as comfortable on your gymnast's feet.

Instruct your gymnast to stand with their back to the spotting block and facing an opened area that is padded.

Next, have your gymnast place their hands on the floor and then one foot on the block. Once your gymnast has one foot on the block, they can then place their other foot on the block. Your gymnast can also place part of their shin on the block if it is more comfortable for them.

Now your gymnast should be in a high elevated push up position with their feet on the block.

Your gymnast's legs, hips, and chest should remain off the floor for this planche drill.

Next, instruct your gymnast to start with their body straight, but not sagging or arched.

Once your gymnast is in the push up position instruct them to move their hands closer to the spotting block and their shoulders forward. Your gymnast should be in a planche position with their feet on the block. Their shoulders should be further from the block than their hands.

Once your gymnast is in the planche position with their shoulders beyond their hands, instruct them to squeeze their buttocks.

Once they have their buttocks squeezed instruct your gymnast to pull their belly button in just as if they were lifting their belly button off the floor in the **Belly Button Lift.** (P. 31)

You should see the lower portion of your gymnast's back elongate into the correct position for a handstand.

# Gymnastics Drills and Conditioning
## For the Handstand

Once your gymnast squeezes their buttocks and then pulls in their belly button they will have performed the "pelvic tilt" in a planche push up position.

After your gymnast has formed the correct shape with their lower body, instruct them to push down on the floor and pull in their chest simultaneously.

The portion of your gymnast's back between their shoulder blades should rise toward the ceiling. Your gymnast has just performed a "shoulder shrug" in the planche push up position with their upper body elevated.

To help teach the shoulder shrug touch the portion of your gymnast's back that is between their shoulder blades and ask them to push up on your hand to form the rounded position.

They are now ready to start the **Planche – Virtual Handstand – Planche** drill.

Instruct your gymnast to hold that tight shape throughout the rest of the **Planche – Virtual Handstand – Planche** drill.

To begin the drill, instruct your gymnast to lift one of their feet\legs to a handstand position and keep their other shin on the block. Your gymnast's entire body, with the exception of the leg still supported on the block should have moved as one unit up to the single leg, or virtual, handstand.

Inform your gymnast that their hips and shoulders should be square with the block and their handstand shape should be correct with the exception of the leg supported by the block. Your gymnast's buttocks should be under, their belly in, their hips open, their chest in, and their shoulders in a shrug position. For this portion of the drill, have your gymnast look at the bottom of the block.

Your gymnast's shoulders, hips, and one ankle should be directly above their hands at this point while the other leg should be supported on the block. The leg that is pointed toward the ceiling should be the one forming the handstand shape with the upper body.

Once your gymnast is in the correct single leg, or virtual, handstand position they can begin the motion for the drill by slowly lowering their free leg back to the block and shifting their

## Shape in Motion

weight forward so they are in a slight planche position. Your gymnast should now be in the elevated push up position, but with their shoulders beyond their finger tips at this point. Instruct your gymnast to look at the floor and to keep their head in line with their spine, neither tucked in nor tilted back. They are in the planche position.

Next, instruct your gymnast to return to the single leg, or virtual, handstand position by lifting their free leg back up above their hips so they are vertical, with the exception of their supported leg. They must also open their armpits back up, and square their shoulders and hips with the block. They will need to bring their shoulders and head into alignment for the correct handstand shape again. It may be easier for your gymnast if you instruct them to look at the floor just above their hands for the planche and then at the center of the block for their handstand.

Once your gymnast understands the motion of the virtual handstand to the planche and back to the virtual handstand, ask them if they can perform a few repetitions before stopping. Inform your gymnast not to planche too far forward until they build strength and become very comfortable so they do not collapse.

You must also inform your gymnast to communicate when they are fatigued and should allow them to rest.

One repetition includes the planche, up to the virtual handstand, and then the return to the planche position.

It is just as important for your gymnast to keep the correct shape and remain tight during the planche as it is for them to keep the correct shape and remain tight in the handstand. Your gymnast must remain tight during the movement from one position to the next.

Constantly remind your gymnast to keep the pelvic tilt, their buttocks squeezed, their chest in, and their arms straight (not locked in the elbows) throughout the entire drill.

Be sure your gymnast's legs remain straight and their feet remain pointed throughout this drill.

# Gymnastics Drills and Conditioning
# For the Handstand

Have your gymnast relax and then repeat this drill a few times if they are able.

Make sure your gymnast starts straight, performs the pelvic tilt, buttocks squeeze, and the shrug before they move into the single leg handstand position and then begin to move to and from the planche position.

This drill, when performed correctly closely simulates a cast handstand on uneven bars. It should help tremendously with Cast Handstand and Clear Hip work on uneven bars.

This exercise puts tremendous pressure on your gymnast's wrists and shoulders. You should allow them to stop this drill when their wrists and shoulders become uncomfortable. Be careful not to allow your gymnast to perform too many repetitions of this drill.

Once your gymnast has mastered this drill in the natural\over grip position, they can attempt this drill in an under grip position to help them prepare for front giant work on uneven bars.

The constant change in shoulder angle causes a change in the demand on your gymnast's upper body muscles. Your gymnast may eventually develop strength in a wider range of positions after performing this drill over the course of time. This drill can help tremendously with Cast Handstand and Clear Hip work on uneven bars.

# Shape in Motion

Have your gymnast start this drill with their hands on the floor.

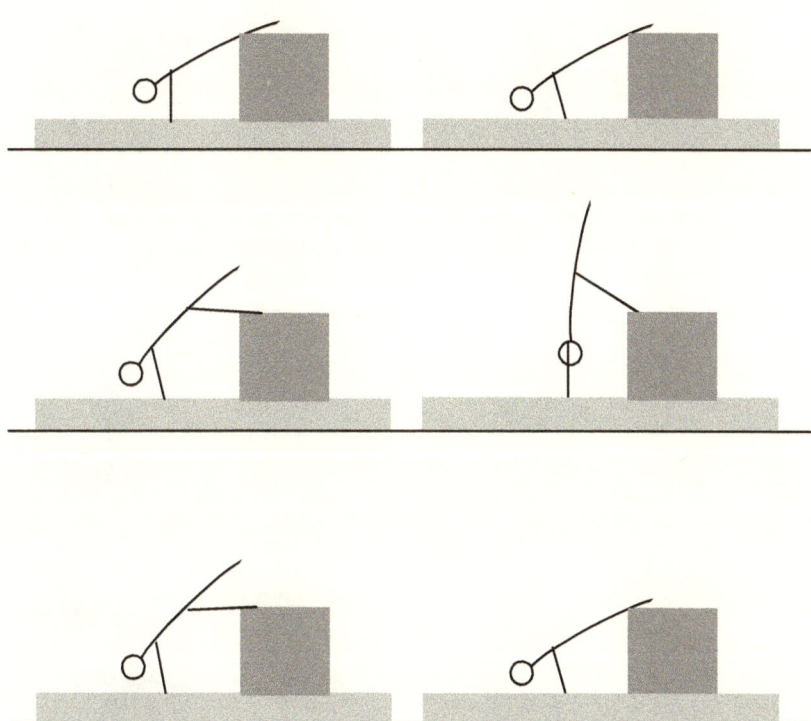

# Gymnastics Drills and Conditioning
## For the Handstand

As your gymnast advances they can place their hands on a floor bar as shown on the next page.

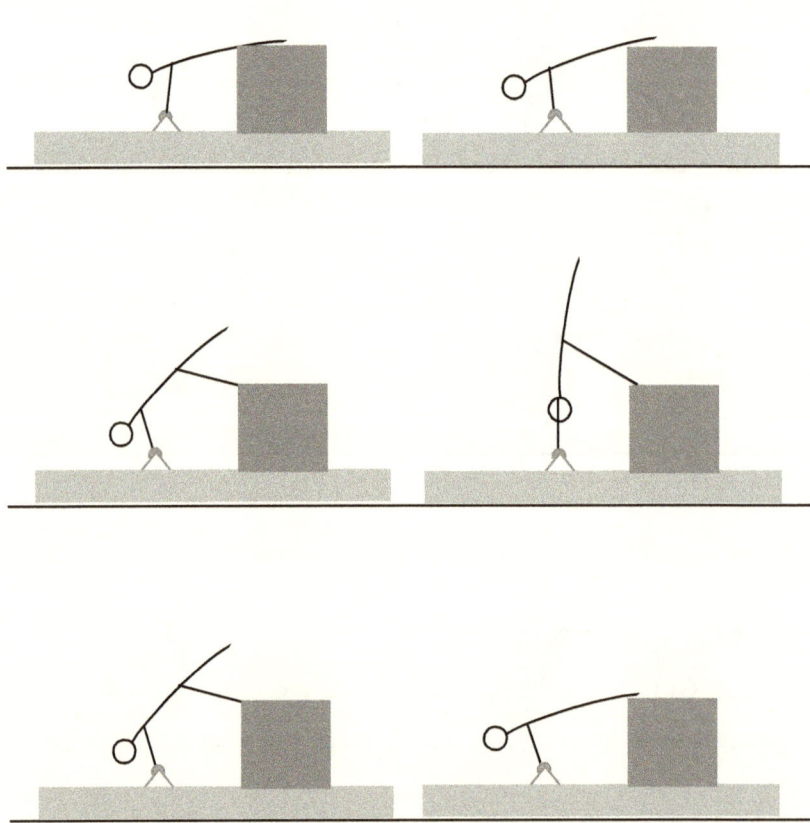

Shape in Motion

**Handstand – Shoulder Open and Close**
This is a shoulder control and planche drill as well as additional training on body tightness and handstand shape.
You must spot your gymnast for this drill from start to finish.
We are going to start this drill from the **Rainbow to Handstand** drill (P. 71) in order to incorporate more body tightness and shape instruction. You can go directly to the handstand, but we encourage coaches and gymnasts to spend a substantial amount of time and energy on handstand work and body tightness.
Inform your gymnast that once they are in the handstand they will be required to remain in the handstand for a substantial amount of time, long enough to focus on shape, body tightness, and shoulder movements.
Give your gymnast full instructions before beginning this drill.
Have your gymnast lie on their stomach, face down.
Use the floor exercise area or a firm mat.
Once your gymnast is on the floor, have them place their hands up by their armpits, so they can push up to a support, a push up position. Your gymnast's legs, hips, and chest all come up off the floor once they are in the push up position.
Instruct your gymnast to point their feet rather than keeping them flexed with the ball of their feet on the floor. Keeping their feet pointed puts more of a demand on your gymnast's abdominal muscles.
Next, instruct your gymnast to start with their body straight, but not sagging or arched.
Once your gymnast is completely straight, instruct them to walk their hands out enough so that their arms are nearly touching their ears. It will be a very long hand support position.
Once your gymnast is long and straight, instruct them to squeeze their buttocks.
Once in the very long hand support position with their buttocks squeezed, instruct your gymnast to pull their belly button in just as if they were lifting their belly button off the floor in the **Belly Button Lift.** (P. 31)
You should see the lower portion of your gymnast's back elongate into the correct position for a handstand.

# Gymnastics Drills and Conditioning For the Handstand

Once your gymnast squeezes their buttocks and then pulls in their belly button they will have performed the "pelvic tilt" on their hands and in the rainbow position.

After your gymnast has formed the correct shape with their lower body, instruct them to push down on the floor and pull in their chest simultaneously.

The portion of your gymnast's back between the shoulder blades should rise toward the ceiling. Your gymnast has just performed a **"shoulder shrug"** in the rainbow position! This shape is called a rainbow because it looks like a long rainbow. Instruct your gymnast to keep their shoulders slightly higher than their buttocks.

To help teach the shrug touch the portion of your gymnast's back that is between their shoulder blades and ask them to push up on your hand to form the rounded position.

Be sure your gymnast's head remains neutral throughout the exercise.

Be sure your gymnast's legs remain straight throughout the exercise.

Next instruct your gymnast to hold that tight shape throughout the rest of the drill.

Once your gymnast is informed, start to lift their heels toward the ceiling.

You will actually need to lift your gymnast by their shins, not by their toes, thighs, belly, or hips.

Lift your gymnast's feet slowly because if they lose the shape you must lower them back to the rainbow position to correct the shape and then make another attempt at the **Rainbow to Handstand**.

Each time your gymnast performs the **Rainbow to Handstand** they must be returned to the Rainbow. It is just as important for your gymnast to keep the correct shape and remain tight on the way down as it was for them to keep the correct shape and remain tight on the way up.

When you are lifting your gymnast's shins toward the ceiling, gently shift their weight forward rather than pulling them away from their hands in order to prevent them from collapsing.

## Shape in Motion

Constantly remind your gymnast to keep the pelvic tilt, their buttocks squeezed, and their chest in throughout the entire drill. Be sure your gymnast's head remains neutral throughout the exercise.

Once your gymnast is successful in completing the **Rainbow to Handstand** we can perform the **Handstand – Shoulder Open and Close**.

For the **Handstand – Open Shoulder and Close**, instruct your gymnast to pull their belly button in as if they are performing the **Belly Button Lift**. (P. 31)

Next instruct them to squeeze their buttocks and watch for their lower back to remain in the elongated or pelvic tilt position. Have your gymnast shrug their shoulders and remind them to pull in their chest if necessary.

Instruct your gymnast to push their toes up toward the ceiling as they did when they performed the **Handstand Shrug without the Wall** drill.

If your gymnast is able to successfully push up you should see their ears rise up to their shoulders. There should be no space between your gymnast's ears and shoulders if they have completely and correctly performed the shrug.

Now instruct your gymnast to keep the tight handstand position and then to slowly open their shoulder angle and then press their armpits out.

Your gymnast's upper body will be in a slight arched position, but their lower body should remain tight and in the correct handstand shape, **Buttocks Squeeze** and **Belly Button Lift**.

To make it easier for your gymnast to understand, instruct them to look for the ceiling while pressing their armpits out.

Once your gymnast's shoulders are stretched so their armpits are completely opened, instruct your gymnast to pull their armpits back in so their shoulders return to the correct handstand position.

Instruct your gymnast to shrug their shoulders so that their ears are hidden by their shoulders. Remember, there should be no space between your gymnast's ears and shoulders if they have completely and correctly performed the shrug in the handstand.

# Gymnastics Drills and Conditioning
## For the Handstand

Make sure your gymnast's handstand shape is correct and your gymnast's body is tight before moving to the next portion of this drill.

For the next portion of this drill ask your gymnast to planche forward by completely pulling their armpits in and pressing the top of their head and their shoulders towards the wall behind them.

Once your gymnast begins to press their shoulders out instruct them to rock forward as they did in the **Planche Drill – Rock Forward and Back**. (P. 75)

It may be easier for your gymnast to understand the planche position if your instruct them to look for the floor just above their finger tips.

Your gymnast's chest should be above or beyond their finger tips for the planche position.

Once the planche position is reached instruct your gymnast to return to the correct handstand shape by pulling their head back into alignment with their shoulders. Remind them to perform the **Belly Button Lift**, **Buttocks Squeeze**, and **Shoulder Shrug**.

One repetition of this drill includes the check for the correct handstand shape, the complete opening of your gymnast's shoulders, returning to the correct handstand shape, the planche, and returning to the correct handstand shape again.

This drill requires your gymnast to be on their hands for a substantial amount of time. Allow them to rest once their wrists and shoulders begin to feel uncomfortable.

Once your gymnast understands the motion, instruct them to initiate and control the open and close of the shoulders as well as the planche and return movement. You must still completely spot your gymnast for this drill even though they are initiating the movements.

**Take precautions**... The movements should be slow and controlled. Many gymnasts do not have very flexible shoulders. Only have your gymnast press out as much as they can comfortably do so in order to prevent collapse or injury. Be sure your gymnast does

## Shape in Motion

not to planche too far forward until they develop strength and confidence in the position.

Be sure your gymnast's legs remain straight and their feet remain pointed throughout the exercise.

This is a shoulder control and planche drill as well as additional instruction on body tightness and handstand shape.

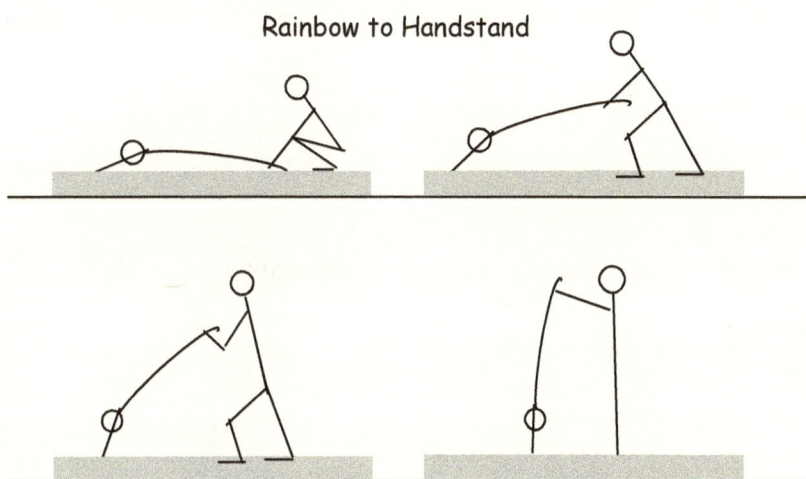

Rainbow to Handstand

# Gymnastics Drills and Conditioning For the Handstand

### Handstand to Open Armpits

### Back to Handstand then to Planche

### Planche and Back to Handstand

Your gymnast's hands do not move during this drill. Many coaches do move back and forth while spotting this drill.

# Quick Handstand Review

Completely Vertical
Upside Down
Belly Button Pulled In
Buttocks Squeezed
Low Back Elongated
Chest In
Shoulders Stretched\Shrugged
No Space between Arms and Ears
Head Neutral
Legs Straight
Legs Together
Feet Pointed

**Best of luck with your training!**

## Other books by this author...

**Gymnastics Drills and Conditioning Exercises**
ISBN: 9781411605794

**Gymnastics Drills and Conditioning for the Handstand**
ISBN: 9781411650008

**Gymnastics Drills: Walkover, Limber, Back Handspring**
ISBN: 9781411611603

**Gymnastics Conditioning for the Legs and Ankles**
ISBN: 9781411620339

**Gymnastics Journal: My Scores, My Goals, My Dreams**
ISBN: 9781411641457

**Most Frequently Asked Questions about Gymnastics**
ISBN: 1591133726

**Fitness Journal: Goals, Training, and Success**
ISBN: 9781847284440

**Strength Training Journal**
ISBN: Not yet assigned.

**Gymnastics Conditioning: Five Conditioning Workouts**
ISBN: 9780615147598

**Swing Set Workouts**
ISBN: 9780615151700

**Fitness on a Swing Set**
ISBN: 9780615147888

**Fitness on a Swing Set with Training Programs**
ISBN: 9780615150284

To order more copies of this book and the other books by this author visit www.GymnasticsStuff.com.

www.GymnasticsDrills.com

# Gymnastics Drills and Conditioning
# For the Handstand

www.ingramcontent.com/pod-product-compliance
Lightning Source LLC
Chambersburg PA
CBHW032008080426
42735CB00007B/543